ites

For Jenny, the love of my life.
Jackson the courageous. Christian the valiant.
Jane the tender. Elle the steadfast. Jones the bold.
And the last one—what gift will you bring?

—D. B.

To Mom and Dad—
apparently my time spent reverently drawing
during sacrament meeting has finally paid off.
And for the record, I was listening.

—R. J.

Text © 2014 David Butler
Illustrations © 2014 Ryan Jeppesen

Visit us at DeseretBook.com

Library of Congress Cataloging-in-Publication Data

Butler, David (Seminary teacher), author.
  Ites : an illustrated guide to the people of The Book of Mormon / David Butler ; illustrated by Ryan Jeppesen.
    pages cm
  Includes bibliographical references.
  ISBN 978-1-60907-938-3 (hardbound : alk. paper)
1. Book of Mormon—Biography. I. Jeppesen, Ryan, illustrator. II. Title.
  BX8627.3.B88 2014
  289.3'22—dc23   2014015258

Printed in China   7/2014
R. R. Donnelley, Shenzhen, Guangdong, China

10   9   8   7   6   5   4   3   2   1

ites

an illustrated guide
to the people in the **Book** of **Mormon**

Written by David Butler

Illustrated by Ryan Jeppesen

DESERET BOOK

Salt Lake City, Utah

Contents

Meet the ites

The people of the Book of Mormon lived centuries ago, but they left a remarkable legacy that still teaches and influences us today. There were men and women of courage and valor—true disciples of Jesus Christ. Others chose to rebel and brought sorrow to their own lives and the lives of people around them. This book highlights some of the stories and lessons from these heroes and villains of the past. Their examples—good and bad—can help you in the trials and decisions that you and your family face every day.

Have you ever pictured what the people of the Book of Mormon looked like? Have you ever wondered what they lived for? What if you applied their stories to your own life? Maybe you can.

Time line of the ites

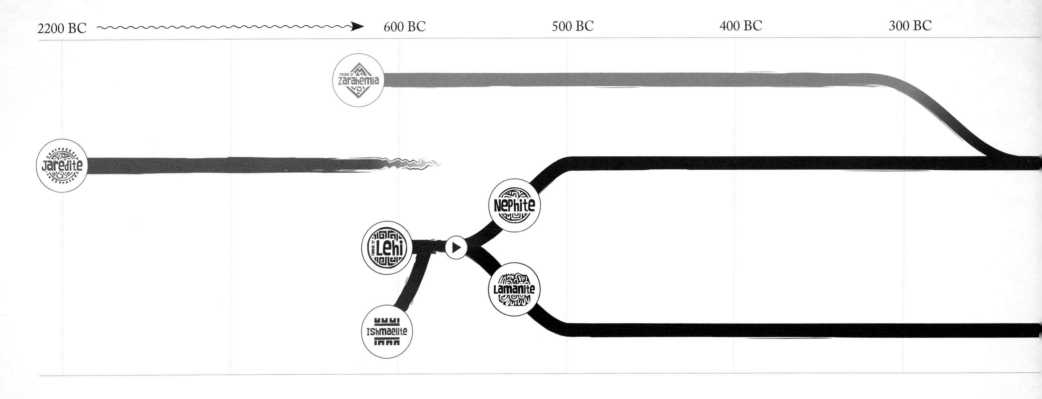

2200 BC ～～～～～→ 600 BC   500 BC   400 BC   300 BC

Jaredite

The **Jaredites** were followers of Jared who fled from the Tower of Babel and were guided by the Lord to the Americas. The Jaredite people lived on the American continent before dying out around the same time that Lehi's family arrived from Jerusalem. The last Jaredite king, Coriantumr, lived to see the final destruction of his people before joining the people of Zarahemla.

PEOPLE OF Zarahemla

The **people of Zarahemla** were also known as the Mulekites. They left Jerusalem at about the same time as Lehi's family, around the year 600 B.C. Their leader, Mulek, was the son of the Jewish king Zedekiah. The Mulekites sailed across the ocean and founded the city Zarahemla. Around 180 B.C., the Mulekites merged with the Nephites and appointed Mosiah I as their new king.

FAMILY OF Lehi

The **Lehites**, or family of Lehi, left Jerusalem around 600 B.C. under the leadership of their father, the prophet Lehi. The Lord warned Lehi to depart with his family before the city was destroyed by the Babylonians. The family traveled through the wilderness and then crossed the ocean before arriving in the promised land. The family eventually divided into the Nephites and the Lamanites.

Ishmaelite

The **Ishmaelites** were descendants of Ishmael, who joined Lehi's family as they fled Jerusalem. When the Nephites and Lamanites separated, some of Ishmael's children decided to join with Laman and Lemuel. From that point, the Ishmaelites were generally grouped with the Lamanites. One notable descendant of Ishmael was King Lamoni, who was converted to the Lord after being taught the gospel by Ammon.

NePhite

The **Nephites** were the followers of Nephi, the son of the prophet Lehi. After the death of Lehi in the promised land, the family split into two groups. Those who chose to follow the prophet Nephi were known as Nephites. The Nephites were made up of smaller groups such as the Jacobites and Josephites. Throughout most of the Book of Mormon, the Nephites were known for their righteousness. However, they eventually fell into unbelief and wickedness and were destroyed by the Lamanites.

Lamanite

The **Lamanites** were the followers of Laman, the prophet Lehi's oldest son. After Lehi's family reached the promised land, the family divided into two groups, the Lamanites and the Nephites. The Lamanites were usually fighting against the Nephites and were known for their wickedness. However, after Jesus Christ visited the American continent, the Lamanites and Nephites lived in peace for nearly 200 years. Eventually, this peace ended and the Lamanites destroyed the Nephites.

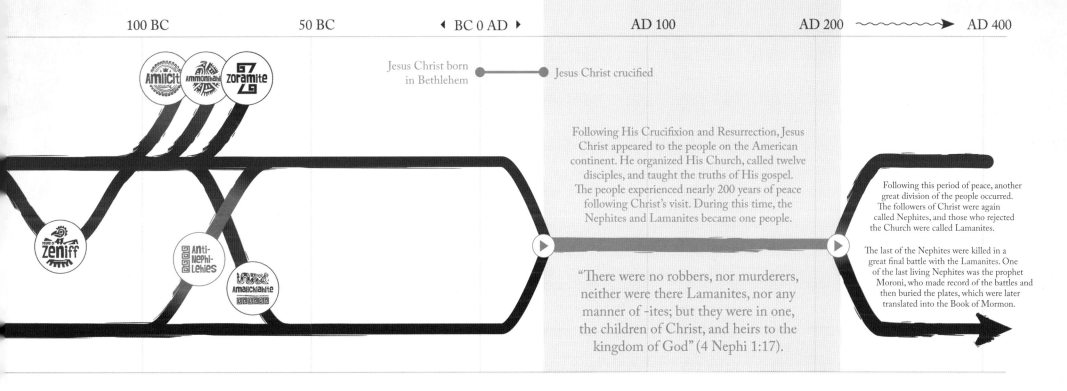

100 BC 50 BC ◀ BC 0 AD ▶ AD 100 AD 200 ～～～➤ AD 400

Jesus Christ born in Bethlehem — Jesus Christ crucified

Following His Crucifixion and Resurrection, Jesus Christ appeared to the people on the American continent. He organized His Church, called twelve disciples, and taught the truths of His gospel. The people experienced nearly 200 years of peace following Christ's visit. During this time, the Nephites and Lamanites became one people.

"There were no robbers, nor murderers, neither were there Lamanites, nor any manner of -ites; but they were in one, the children of Christ, and heirs to the kingdom of God" (4 Nephi 1:17).

Following this period of peace, another great division of the people occurred. The followers of Christ were again called Nephites, and those who rejected the Church were called Lamanites.

The last of the Nephites were killed in a great final battle with the Lamanites. One of the last living Nephites was the prophet Moroni, who made record of the battles and then buried the plates, which were later translated into the Book of Mormon.

The people of Zeniff were a group of Nephites who followed their leader, Zeniff, and separated from the Nephites during the time of King Mosiah I to return to the original land of Nephi. At the time, the land was inhabited by Lamanites. The Zeniffites lived peacefully among the Lamanites for many years, but they were brought into captivity during the reign of Zeniff's grandson, King Limhi. The group was discovered by Ammon, a servant of King Mosiah II. They then returned to live with the Nephites in the land of Zarahemla.

The Amlicites were a group of Nephite dissenters led by Amlici. Amlici sought to become king of the Nephites but was defeated by the voice of the people. When this attempt failed, he and his followers waged war against the Nephites and later joined forces with the Lamanites. The Amlicite-Lamanite army was soon defeated by the Nephites, and Amlici was killed during the battle.

The Ammonihahites were a group of wicked Nephites who lived in the city of Ammonihah, an apostate Nephite city. The prophet Alma taught and was persecuted in the city of Ammonihah with his companion Amulek. The entire city of Ammonihah and its people were destroyed by the Lamanites.

Anti-Nephi-Lehies

The Anti-Nephi-Lehies were a group of Lamanites who converted to God's Church after being taught by Ammon and the other sons of Mosiah. They lived in the kingdom of Lamoni's father and adopted the name of Anti-Nephi-Lehies after their conversion to the gospel. Their Lamanite neighbors who did not convert became angry with them and continued to wage war against them. The group left the Lamanite lands after their conversion and joined with the Nephites.

Zoramite

The Zoramites were an apostate group of Nephites during the reign of the judges and ministry of Alma the Younger. They were named after their leader, Zoram. They were known for their strange form of worship and their prideful behavior. This group shouldn't be confused with Zoram, the servant of Laban, who left Jerusalem with the family of Lehi in the year 600 B.C.

The Amalickiahites were Nephite apostates named after their leader, Amalickiah. Amalickiah wanted to be king of the Nephites, but Captain Moroni gathered an army to stop him. Amalickiah took a small number of men and joined the Lamanites. Through cunning and murder, he eventually became the Lamanite king. Following several battles with Captain Moroni's Nephite armies, Amalickiah was killed by Teancum.

Lehi

The Book of Mormon begins with the journey of the prophet Lehi and his family from the city of Jerusalem to the promised land. Lehi was married to Sariah, and they were the parents of Laman, Lemuel, Sam, Nephi, Jacob, Joseph, and some daughters, whose names aren't recorded in the Book of Mormon. The Lord commanded Lehi to warn the people to repent or the city of Jerusalem would be destroyed, but the people became angry and tried to kill Lehi. The Lord spoke to Lehi in a dream and commanded him to lead his family out of Jerusalem before the city was destroyed. Lehi and his family remained faithful and obedient, and the Lord watched over and protected them. He led Lehi through the wilderness and across the ocean and gave him many instructions, visions, and revelations.

 Lehi was not the only prophet in Jerusalem at the time he was called. The Lord called many prophets during the time Lehi lived there, including Jeremiah.

 The Lord commanded Lehi and his family to leave Jerusalem in 600 BC. They did not arrive in the promised land until about 590 BC.

 The brass plates contained a record of Lehi's genealogy. He was a descendant of Joseph who was sold into Egypt.

 Lehi was a wealthy man when he lived in Jerusalem, but he left all of his riches behind when the Lord commanded him to leave.

 "Therefore, I would that ye should know, that after the Lord had shown so many marvelous things unto my father, Lehi, . . . he went forth among the people, and began to prophesy and to declare unto them concerning the things which he had both seen and heard" (1 Nephi 1:18).

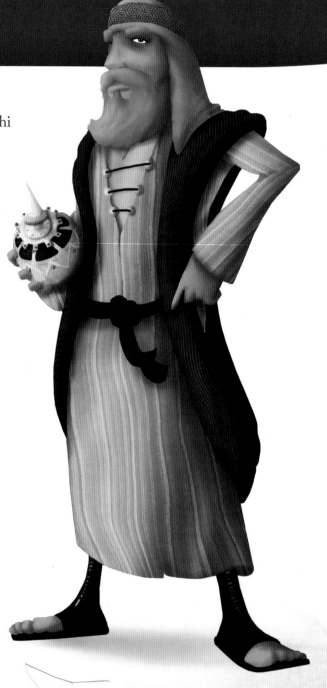

Guided by God (1 Nephi 1–17)

Lehi was commanded by the Lord to lead his family through the wilderness and to the promised land because the city of Jerusalem was in danger due to the people's wickedness. This would require Lehi and his family to exercise great faith. They did not know where the Lord was leading them. As the family traveled, Lehi received instructions from the Lord about where to go and when to stop. He was given the Liahona, a compass that pointed the direction the family should travel and provided special instructions when needed. Every time the Lord gave directions, Lehi followed them. Lehi's instructions to his children often began with the same phrase:

"Wherefore, the Lord hath commanded me."

(1 Nephi 3:4)

Lehi continually asked the Lord where his family should go and what they should do. He was protected and blessed because he listened to and followed the promptings of the Lord.

Each of us is traveling through the wilderness of life. We do not know what dangers or opportunities lie ahead. With so many opinions and voices in the world, we might be confused about which way we should go. The Lord can guide us like He guided Lehi.

? Will you be like Lehi and diligently try to hear the voice of the Lord? Will you look to Him for directions and advice in your life? Will you follow His instructions when they come?

Activity

Set up a mini obstacle course in your home or outside. Choose one person to blindfold, and ask him or her to try to navigate through the obstacle course. As the blindfolded person makes his or her way through the course, have most of the group shout different directions and bad advice about where to go. Select one member of the group to whisper the right way to go. Tell the person traveling through the obstacle course to try to listen to and follow the directions of the quiet voice in order to make it through.

Sariah

Sariah was the wife of the prophet Lehi and the mother of the prophet Nephi. The Lord commanded her family to leave their home in Jerusalem and to travel through the wilderness and across the sea to the promised land. Lehi and Sariah were the parents of six sons (Laman, Lemuel, Sam, Nephi, Jacob, and Joseph) and some daughters. Sariah experienced many trials and hardships while her family traveled in the wilderness for many years, but she remained faithful. When given the choice to stay in her comfortable life or follow the Lord, she chose the Lord.

 Sariah was a wealthy woman when she lived in Jerusalem.

 Jacob and Joseph, Sariah's youngest sons, were born while the family journeyed in the wilderness.

 Sariah is one of only a few women mentioned by name in the Book of Mormon.

 Sariah nearly died during the voyage across the ocean.

 "And it came to pass that they did rejoice exceedingly, and did offer sacrifice . . . unto the Lord" (1 Nephi 5:9).

The Cost of Obedience (1 Nephi 2–5)

Following the Lord's command to leave Jerusalem would require a major lifestyle change for Lehi's family. Sariah made the decision to follow the Lord by trusting in and following her husband. She left her home, her gold, her silver, and the comfortable life she had enjoyed in the city to raise her family in a tent in the desert wilderness. On two occasions, the Lord sent her sons back to Jerusalem with special missions. She had to say good-bye without knowing if she would see them again. She exercised great trust and sacrificed much in order to follow the Lord. When her sons returned safely, she testified:

"I also know of a surety that the Lord hath protected my sons, and delivered them." (1 Nephi 5:8)

We do not always know the reasons behind the things the Lord asks of us. Listening to and obeying His commands often requires us to give up something. Following the Lord requires sacrifice.

? Will you show the same level of trust that Sariah did when the Lord asks you to sacrifice and to obey?

Activity

Have each person bring one of his or her favorite possessions to show the group. Go around the circle and have each person explain why it would be hard to give that item up, and then invite people to testify of the importance of sacrifice and to explain why following the Lord is more important than earthly possessions.

Nephi

Nephi is the first writer in the Book of Mormon. He is the son of the prophet Lehi and his wife, Sariah, and is the younger brother of Laman, Lemuel, and Sam and the older brother of Jacob and Joseph. The Book of Mormon begins with Nephi telling the story of his family's journey from Jerusalem after God commanded Lehi to take his family into the wilderness. Although Nephi was one of the younger brothers, the Lord chose him to be a leader in his family due to his righteousness. During Nephi's journey, the Lord commanded him to build a ship that would take his family to the promised land. This great prophet and leader left a great legacy—the descendants of Nephi and those who joined them in following the Lord called themselves Nephites.

 Nephi was young when his family left Jerusalem in 600 BC. He may have still been in his teenage years.

 Nephi married a daughter of Ishmael, a man who brought his family with Lehi into the wilderness.

 The Lord commanded Nephi to build a temple when they got to the promised land. It was designed like Solomon's temple in Jerusalem.

 The First and Second Books of Nephi are primarily written by this Nephi. Several other men named Nephi come later in the Book of Mormon, such as the Nephi that lived when the Savior visited the promised land in AD 34.

 "As the Lord liveth, and as we live, we will not go down . . . until we have accomplished the thing which the Lord hath commanded us" (1 Nephi 3:15).

No Matter What (1 Nephi 3–4, 16–18)

From the time Nephi was young, the Lord asked him to do difficult things.

He was commanded to leave his home in Jerusalem, to travel and live in tents in the wilderness, to get the brass plates from the wicked Laban, to build a boat, to cross the ocean, to establish a city, and to be a leader and teacher to his rebellious older brothers.

Whenever the Lord spoke, Nephi responded in faith and obedience.

"I will go and do the things which the Lord hath commanded." (1 Nephi 3:7)

Many times during his life, Nephi ran into obstacles. There were plenty of times when it might have been easier to quit. When Nephi and his brothers followed the Lord's command to try to get the brass plates from Laban, they were threatened, had all of their treasure stolen, and had to run for their lives from Laban's soldiers. Laman and Lemuel wanted to give up—but not Nephi. He was committed to keeping God's commandments, no matter what.

There will be times when the Lord will ask you to do something hard. When these times come, you might be tempted to give up.

? Are you committed to obeying all of God's commandments? What will you do when the journey is difficult? Will you give up? Or will you live like Nephi and accomplish all that the Lord asks of you?

Activity

Play "Simon Says" to practice exact obedience. Try to use actions that would be similar to some of the things Nephi did. For example, "Simon says, pretend to build a boat." Or, "Simon says, tiptoe as if you're sneaking into a city."

Laman and Lemuel

Lamanite

Laman and Lemuel are the oldest sons of the prophet Lehi and his wife, Sariah. They are the older brothers to Sam, Nephi, Jacob, and Joseph. Laman and Lemuel traveled with Lehi and the rest of the family when the Lord commanded them to leave Jerusalem, but they caused trouble the entire time. Laman and Lemuel were upset about leaving their lifestyle and money in Jerusalem. Throughout the entire journey, they complained, lied, acted wickedly, hurt their family members, and even tried to kill Nephi and Lehi. Though they sometimes briefly repented and tried to follow the Lord, most of the time they were rebellious. They even taught their children to hate Nephi and his family.

 The people in the Book of Mormon known as the Lamanites are descendants of Laman and Lemuel and are generally known for their wickedness, though they sometimes were righteous.

 Under Israelite law, Laman, the oldest son, should have been the ruler over the family when Lehi died, but he disqualified himself due to his wickedness.

 Laman and Lemuel resented their younger brother Nephi for becoming their leader, and their hatred was passed down through many generations.

 "And he also spake unto Lemuel: O that thou mightest be like unto this valley, firm and steadfast, and immovable in keeping the commandments of the Lord!" (1 Nephi 2:10).

Murmur, Murmur (1 Nephi 2–17)

Many of the problems that Lehi's family experienced on their journey were either caused or made worse by Laman and Lemuel. When the Lord commanded the family to leave Jerusalem, Laman and Lemuel murmured. When the Lord asked Lehi's sons to return to Jerusalem to get the brass plates, Laman and Lemuel complained. When their tasks were hard, Laman and Lemuel gave up. When they witnessed miracles, they denied them. When they were tired, hungry, or angry, they took it out on others.

Lehi and Nephi constantly tried to help Laman and Lemuel by teaching them truth and pleading with them to trust in the Lord.

"And thus Laman and Lemuel, being the eldest, did murmur against their father. And they did murmur because they knew not the dealings of that God who had created them." (1 Nephi 2:12)

Life in the wilderness was certainly difficult, but Laman and Lemuel made the situation even more difficult by the way they approached their problems. They missed out on the great blessings the Lord was providing because they were so focused on themselves. Many generations of people suffered due to Laman and Lemuel's bad decisions.

It is easy in life to complain, disbelieve, and be hurtful to others. These actions lead to sadness. You can choose positive ways to respond in difficult situations.

? What kind of life will you live? Will you complain and blame others, or will you trust in God and face the future with faith, hope, and a loving heart?

Activity

Set a goal in your family to go one week without complaining. Resolve to make an extra effort to be positive. Keep a jar in an open place in the house, and put a piece of candy or a penny in it every time someone speaks positively, compliments someone, shows gratitude, or is helpful. See if you can fill the jar!

Sam

 **NePhite**

Sam was the third son of the prophet Lehi and his wife, Sariah. He was a younger brother of Laman and Lemuel and an older brother of Nephi, Jacob, and Joseph. When the Lord commanded Lehi's sons to get the brass plates from Laban, Sam faithfully went. He also returned to Jerusalem with his brothers to bring Ishmael's family to join Lehi's on their journey. In all of these experiences, Sam followed, trusted in, and or defended Nephi. When the family divided into separate groups in the promised land, Sam and his family followed Nephi.

 Many people think Sam was younger than Nephi, but he was actually older.

 Out of the older brothers, Sam is mentioned the least in the Book of Mormon.

 Sam married a daughter of Ishmael, and his family remained faithful during their lives.

 Sam and his family were promised the same great blessings that Lehi prophesied would come to Nephi and his family.

 "And I spake unto Sam, making known unto him the things which the Lord had manifested unto me by his Holy Spirit. And it came to pass that he believed in my words" (1 Nephi 2:17).

Consistently Faithful (1 Nephi 2–17)

Many people might not remember much about Sam when they finish reading the Book of Mormon. Sam often seems to stay in the background. When Nephi, Sam's younger brother, was called by the Lord to be a leader over the family, Nephi's other older brothers, Laman and Lemuel, rebelled. But Sam faithfully followed Nephi without complaint. Sam was not in charge, but that didn't stop him from always obeying the Lord's commands. His prayers and love for Nephi must have been a great strength to him.

Sam was not in the spotlight, but he was always faithful. The Lord knew that He could trust Sam to be faithful and obedient in every way. He promised Sam the same blessings promised to his prophet brother, Nephi.

"Blessed art thou, and thy seed; for thou shalt inherit the land like unto they brother Nephi." (2 Nephi 4:11)

Sometimes we want people to notice the good we do. We might feel like the Lord needs and appreciates the leaders of the Church more than the helpers. However, our Heavenly Father loves the "Sams" of the world—those who serve faithfully without any recognition or praise—as much as He loves the "Nephis." Our worth is never dependent upon our calling. It only matters to the Lord that we are committed to our covenants.

? Will you faithfully serve and give like Sam, no matter what part you are asked to play? Will you provide time, strength, and sustaining service without demanding attention or praise in return?

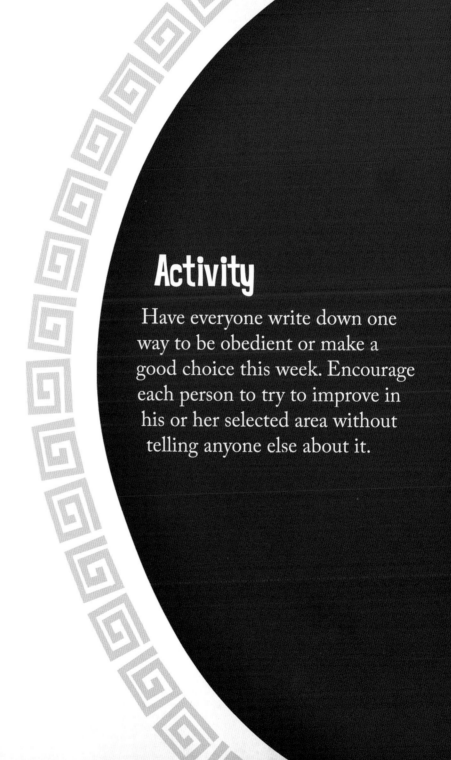

Activity

Have everyone write down one way to be obedient or make a good choice this week. Encourage each person to try to improve in his or her selected area without telling anyone else about it.

Laban

Israelite

Laban was a Jewish elder living in Jerusalem in the days of Lehi and his family. Laban was a leader and was in charge of a group of at least fifty men. He is important in the story of the Book of Mormon because he kept the brass plates—a record of prophets and important family history—in his treasury. After Laban robbed and tried to kill Nephi and his brothers and refused to give them the brass plates, the Lord commanded Nephi to slay him.

 Lehi and Laban both descended from Joseph who was sold into Egypt.

 Zoram, who joined Lehi's family on their journey, was a servant of Laban and a keeper of his treasury.

 Nephi took Laban's sword with him to the promised land and used it as a model for producing more swords.

 Laban met with the elders of the Jews the night he was killed. He seemed to be a man of great importance in Jerusalem.

 "Let us be faithful in keeping the commandments of the Lord; for behold he is mightier than all the earth, then why not mightier than Laban and his fifty, yea, or even than his tens of thousands?" (1 Nephi 4:1).

It Is Better (1 Nephi 3–4)

Laban's refusal to give the holy scriptures to Lehi's family could have prevented thousands of people from receiving happiness and eternal life. Nephi and his brothers tried several different times to reason with Laban, but he stole their property and tried to kill them. The Lord taught Nephi that without the brass plates, the family of Lehi would not have the words of the Lord or know of His covenants and promises.

"It is better that one man should perish than that a nation should dwindle and perish in unbelief." (1 Nephi 4:13)

Nephi and his brothers tried to find peaceful ways to get the plates from Laban, but Laban stubbornly refused. In order to protect his family's spiritual well-being, Nephi had to follow the Lord's command to slay Laban.

Sometimes our stubbornness or selfishness may prevent others from being blessed. The Lord may ask us to give up things in our lives, such as our time, talents, or material possessions, in order to better bless others. It is better to sacrifice the things the Lord asks of us than to dwindle in unbelief or cause others to suffer.

? Is there something in your life that is holding you back spiritually? What can you give up to progress on your journey and help others become more like the Savior?

Activity

Go outside and time how long it takes someone to run a chosen short distance (for example, between two trees). After the first run, tie something heavy to each of the runner's feet and time him or her again. Talk about how these weights represent things in our life that we should let go of in order to better serve the Lord. Discuss what we could do to get rid of them.

Zoram

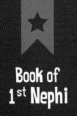

Zoram was a trusted servant of Laban, who was a leader in Jerusalem. One of Zoram's jobs was to watch over and take care of Laban's treasures. Nephi met Zoram the night of Laban's death. After following the command to kill Laban, Nephi put on Laban's clothes and sword as a disguise. He used this disguise to obtain the plates of brass from the treasury. Zoram believed Nephi was Laban, so he gave Nephi the plates and even helped him take them outside the city walls. Zoram never went back to Jerusalem; instead, he joined Lehi's family on their journey. Zoram and his family remained with the Nephites when they reached the promised land.

 Zoram married the oldest daughter of Ishmael. This could signify that he was older than all of Lehi's sons.

 The descendants of Zoram mixed with the descendants of Nephi, Sam, and Jacob and were known as Nephites.

 Zoram was a servant of Laban, but once he left Jerusalem he was considered a part of Lehi's family.

 This Zoram should not be confused with two Zorams found in the Book of Alma. One of them is a Nephite commander, and the other is an apostate who leads a group called Zoramites.

 "I know that thou art a true friend unto my son, Nephi, forever. Wherefore, because thou hast been faithful thy seed shall be blessed with his seed, that they dwell in prosperity long upon the face of this land" (2 Nephi 1:30–31).

A True and Trusted Friend (1 Nephi 4, 2 Nephi 1)

Thinking they had been discovered and were in danger, Nephi's brothers ran away when they saw Zoram and a man they thought was Laban approaching. When Nephi yelled out to calm their fears, Zoram thought *he* was in danger and started to run back to the city. Nephi caught him and quickly promised not to hurt him. He offered Zoram an opportunity to be free from his life as a servant.

"And it came to pass that Zoram did take courage at the words." (1 Nephi 4:35)

When Zoram promised to remain with Lehi's family, he gave his word by an oath, or promise. From that point on, all of the brothers knew they could trust him. Zoram remained a faithful and loyal friend to Nephi his entire life. Lehi told Zoram, "I know that thou art a true friend unto my son, Nephi, forever" (2 Nephi 1:30).

We live in a time of much distrust, lying, and selfishness. It can be hard to find someone you can trust, who will always look after you, and who will help you progress. The world needs more friends like Zoram—friends that give us courage and remain true forever.

? What kind of friend are you? Are your friends safe with you? Do you encourage them and give them strength to become better?

Activity

Organize a three-legged race. Use strips of fabric or another material to tie the left leg of one partner to the right leg of the other partner. Have them race against other partners. Afterward, discuss the importance of having a friend you can trust who will run the race of life with you.

The Family of Ishmael

Ishmaelite

Ishmael and his family play an important role early in the Book of Mormon. After Laman, Lemuel, Nephi, and Sam returned to the family camp in the wilderness with the brass plates, the Lord commanded them to return to Jerusalem again to invite another family to join with them on their journey. The Lord selected Ishmael's family and sent Lehi's sons to their home. The daughters of Ishmael married the sons of Lehi. Ishmael died before the group made their journey across the ocean, but his descendants became a part of history as they helped build the Nephite and Lamanite civilizations.

 Ishmael died in a place called Nahom before the group crossed the ocean. After his death, contention arose among his family.

 Ishmael and his wife had five daughters and two sons.

 We do not know the name of Ishmael's wife, but she showed her valiant character when she defended and tried to protect Nephi when others rebelled against him.

 King Lamoni was a descendant of Ishmael.

 "And it came to pass that the Lord did soften the heart of Ishmael, and also his household, insomuch that they took their journey with us down into the wilderness to the tent of our father" (1 Nephi 7:5).

The Journey Is Worth It (1 Nephi 7)

The Lord first sent the sons of Lehi back to Jerusalem to get the brass plates. After they returned to their camp from that very long and difficult journey, the Lord sent them back to Jerusalem yet again to invite the family of Ishmael to join with them.

"It came to pass that the Lord spake unto him again, saying that it was not meet for him, Lehi, that he should take his family into the wilderness alone." (1 Nephi 7:1)

Perhaps the Lord was teaching the sons and daughters of Lehi the importance of family. He wanted them to know that marrying a spouse and raising faithful children was worth the difficult travel through the dangerous desert. Ishmael's example teaches us that a life in the wilderness with your family is better than a comfortable life without them. The sons of Lehi followed the direction of the Lord in choosing their spouses, and the way they raised their children had long-lasting consequences for generations to come.

The importance of marriage and family has not changed since the day that Nephi went to visit Ishmael and his family. The Lord still needs righteous men to marry righteous women and raise righteous children. The greatest joys of life are still found in families. They are worth the journey.

? How important is your family in your life? What do your actions and words say about how you feel about your family?

Activity

Draw or paint a family tree with enough branches for each member of the family. Cut small leaves, flowers, or fruit out of paper and set them aside. Challenge each member of the family to do kind deeds and to spend quality time with other family members. Each time a person "chooses family," have them put a leaf, flower, or fruit on the tree. See if you can fill the branches!

Jacob

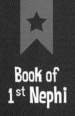

Nephite

Jacob is the fifth son of Lehi and Sariah. His older brothers are Laman, Lemuel, Sam, and Nephi. Jacob was born after the Lord commanded his parents to leave Jerusalem and live in the wilderness. Sariah had two babies while the family journeyed in the wilderness—Jacob and Joseph. They were not born into an easy life. After Lehi died, Nephi led the family and became the group's spiritual leader, and he chose Jacob to be a teacher over the people. The people looked to him for his spiritual strength and righteous example. Jacob frequently mentioned in his writings and speeches how anxious he felt about the spiritual welfare of his people. He truly loved his people and felt responsible for them.

 Jacob's sermons and writings are found in 2 Nephi and in the Book of Jacob.

 Jacob was about fifty-five years old when Nephi gave him care of the plates.

 In the plates, Jacob included an allegory from the prophet Zenos about an olive tree. It is found in Jacob chapter 5, the longest chapter in the Book of Mormon.

 Nephi tells us that his brother Jacob was privileged to see the Savior. One of Jacob's trademarks is his powerful testimony of Christ.

 "O be wise; what can I say more?" (Jacob 6:12).

Protecting the Pure (1 Nephi 2–17)

Jacob and his younger brother, Joseph, were born during a very hard time for their family. Their first years of life were spent in the wilderness, their family having recently escaped from Jerusalem. Many of their troubles came because Laman and Lemuel rebelled and treated their mother and other family members poorly. At one time, Lehi and Sariah nearly died and the younger brothers were sorely grieved because of Laman and Lemuel's actions.

Even though Jacob's life was very difficult, the Lord watched over and protected him as a baby and young boy. Jacob learned that it is important to Heavenly Father that people take care of His daughters and little children. Jacob boldly taught the Nephites and scolded them for mistreating their women and children.

"Also it grieveth me that I must use so much boldness . . . before your wives and your children, many of whose feelings are exceedingly tender and chaste and delicate before God." (Jacob 2:7)

We live in a day when women and children are often treated poorly. This offends our Heavenly Father. He protects and watches over His children, and He commands us to do the same.

? Will you defend the virtue of women in the world? Will you treat your mother, your sisters, and other women with respect and honor? Will you defend the purity and innocence of children wherever you go?

Activity

Have a family discussion about ways you can stand up for women and children. What can you do if you see someone being bullied or teased? How will you react if someone is speaking inappropriately about a woman? Role-play situations like these to practice good ways to respond.

Enos

The Book of Enos is one of the shortest books in the Book of Mormon, but it demonstrates the powerful faith of a man named Enos. Enos's father, Jacob, was a righteous and loving parent who taught Enos the gospel of Jesus Christ and the joy that comes from following Him. Enos probably grew up learning the gospel and the role of the Savior from his parents. His writing focuses on a time when he went on a hunting trip and pondered the truth of the things he had learned from his father and mother. He prayed earnestly to feel forgiveness for his sins and rejoiced when he felt his guilt swept away.

 Enos was the son of Jacob, which made him the nephew of Nephi and the grandson of Lehi and Sariah.

 Enos gave the plates to his son Jarom around 420 BC, 180 years after Lehi left Jerusalem.

 Enos mentioned that there were many wars during his time as well as many prophets among the people.

 The Lamanites became ferocious during Enos's day and wanted to kill the Nephites. Enos prayed diligently for the Lamanites, many of whom were his relatives.

 "And I will tell you of the wrestle which I had before God, before I received a remission of my sins" (Enos 1:2).

My Soul Hungered (Enos)

From a young age, Enos learned from his parents and other leaders about the scriptures, charity, and forgiveness. He came from a family that loved the Lord and His Church. Enos had been taught all of the important facts about the gospel, and he desired to feel a personal witness of their truth deep in his heart. He wrote of a day he spent alone in the wilderness thinking, pondering, and praying.

"And my soul hungered; and I kneeled down before my Maker, and I cried unto him in mighty prayer and supplication for mine own soul; and all the day long did I cry unto him; yea, and when the night came I did still raise my voice high that it reached the heavens." (Enos 1:4)

Enos did not just offer a routine prayer; he humbled himself and poured out his soul to his Heavenly Father. In answer to his plea, Heavenly Father gave Enos his own witness and knowledge of the goodness of God and the power of the Atonement.

We each need to have personal spiritual experiences and to develop a personal relationship with the Lord. We need to find quiet moments to pray sincerely so that Heavenly Father can speak to our hearts and allow us to feel the truth.

? Do you hunger for spiritual experiences the same way you do for food? Do you seek revelation and create opportunities for these spiritual experiences to happen?

Activity

Plan some time for everyone to ponder the gospel truths they have learned and the spiritual experiences they have had. You could play some inspiring music and invite everyone to write their thoughts in a journal or to look at pictures depicting gospel principles. Discuss the importance of creating moments that invite personal revelation.

King Mosiah I

King Mosiah I was a righteous king who reigned over the people of Nephi. His time as king is briefly described in the Book of Omni. Much like Lehi, King Mosiah I was commanded to leave the lands he and his people were living in and to take a journey. All followers of Christ were commanded to leave the land of Nephi and follow King Mosiah I. He and his people discovered a land called Zarahemla, which was filled with another group of people, the Mulekites, who had come to the promised land at about the same time as Lehi. The Mulekites united with the followers of Christ under the righteous leadership of King Mosiah.

 King Mosiah I left the land of Nephi around the year 200 BC.

 The language of the people of Zarahemla had become corrupted and they had no knowledge of God when the Nephites discovered them. King Mosiah I taught them his people's language and the holy scriptures.

 There are two King Mosiahs in the scriptures. King Mosiah I is the father of King Benjamin and the grandfather of King Mosiah II.

 Heavenly Father blessed Mosiah with the gift to interpret languages. King Mosiah I translated a history of the Jaredites from a record contained on a large stone.

 "And they were led by many preachings and prophesyings. And they were admonished continually by the word of God; and they were led by the power of his arm, through the wilderness" (Omni 1:13).

As Many as Would Hearken (Omni 1:12–22)

We do not know how long Mosiah I was king before the Lord commanded him to take his people and depart out of the land of Nephi. Immediately after the Lord's warning to leave, King Mosiah and those who followed the prophet prepared to leave their homes.

"And it came to pass that he did according as the Lord had commanded him. And they departed out of the land into the wilderness, as many as would hearken unto the voice of the Lord." (Omni 1:13)

There were many people who stayed behind in the land of Nephi. Only those who hearkened unto the voice of the Lord and believed in prophecy followed King Mosiah. These faithful disciples did not know where they were going, but they trusted the Lord's servant. They were blessed with amazing spiritual experiences and were able to witness miracles because they chose to follow the Lord's commands.

Today, the Lord still speaks, leads, and warns us through His servants. We may not know all of the reasons we are asked to do certain things, but the outcome will be the same as it was in the days of King Mosiah. We will be protected, blessed with miracles, and given many spiritual experiences when we follow the prophet.

? Will you follow the warnings and teachings of the Lord that come through His chosen servants? Will you trust in living prophets and apostles?

Activity

Using the most recent general conference edition of the *Ensign* magazine or the general conference resources found on LDS.org, have family members select a talk and search for warnings and counsel from the prophets. Family members could do this individually or you could read and summarize a talk together. Make a goal as a family to follow the counsel given.

People of Zarahemla

The people of Zarahemla are introduced in the Book of Omni. Amaleki, one of the book's writers, told the story of King Mosiah I being warned by the Lord to flee from the land of Nephi. After traveling for some time, King Mosiah's people met Zarahemla, a leader of a group that the Nephites had not known existed. The people of Zarahemla were very happy to be joined by the people of Nephi. The Lord had instructed a man named Mulek to lead these people away from Jerusalem around 600 BC. They were living in the promised land at the same time as the Nephites and the Lamanites. The Nephites who had followed Mosiah and the people of Zarahemla united together as one group under the leadership of King Mosiah I.

 Zarahemla was a descendant of Mulek, who was a son of King Zedekiah, the king of Jerusalem when Lehi left and the city was destroyed.

 The people of Zarahemla are also known as the Mulekites.

 Before they met King Mosiah I and his people, the people of Zarahemla met Coriantumr, the last living Jaredite. The Jaredites are another group of people the Lord led to the promised land. Their story is found in the Book of Ether.

 The city of Zarahemla became the capital city of the land and the setting for other significant Book of Mormon events.

 "And at the time that Mosiah discovered them, they had become exceedingly numerous. Nevertheless, they had had many wars and serious contentions, and had fallen by the sword from time to time; and their language had become corrupted; and they had brought no records with them; and they denied the being of their Creator" (Omni 1:17).

Scripture Power (Omni 1:12–22)

Mulek and his people left Jerusalem about the same time as Lehi and his family. Before Lehi's family left the old world, Nephi and his brothers returned to Jerusalem after many days of travel in the wilderness to get the brass plates—their scriptures. They risked their lives and sacrificed their possessions to get the plates. The people of Mulek did not bring any scriptures with them when they came to the new world. By the time King Mosiah I met the people of Zarahemla, their language had become different and they no longer believed in God.

"And also Zarahemla did rejoice exceedingly, because the Lord had sent the people of Mosiah with the plates of brass which contained the record of the Jews." (Omni 1:14)

King Mosiah taught the people of Zarahemla his language and history so they could understand the scriptures. Zarahemla knew how important the scriptures were to the spiritual welfare of his people. Their knowledge of the scriptures converted them to the Lord and caused them to unite with His followers.

Through His prophets and apostles, the Lord continues to emphasize to us today the importance of the scriptures. The conversion of the people of Zarahemla teaches us what a difference the scriptures can make in our lives. Daily scripture study strengthens our faith and increases our testimony.

? Will you continue to make personal and family scripture study an important part of your life? Will you share the scriptures with people you know who are living without their guidance?

Activity

Gather pictures depicting favorite scripture stories. Have each person in the family choose one of the pictures and share what they love about the story and the lesson it teaches. Discuss as a family how life would be different without these great scripture truths and examples.

King Benjamin

King Benjamin was the son of King Mosiah I and was the second king over the people made up of the Nephites and Mulekites. King Benjamin was a wise leader and was beloved by his people. They trusted him and looked to him for spiritual guidance. Just before King Benjamin died, he gathered his people together to teach them the gospel and counsel them to make a covenant with Heavenly Father to take upon themselves the name of Christ. He taught his people from a tall tower, and his teachings had a powerful effect on all who heard it. Before he died, King Benjamin chose his son, Mosiah II, to be the new king over the people.

 King Benjamin reigned until about 120 BC, when he gave his final counsel to the people.

 The words of King Benjamin's famous speech were given to him by an angel.

 King Benjamin was king of the people of Zarahemla at about the same time that King Noah was king of the people in the land of Nephi.

 Amaleki, the writer of part of the book of Omni, had no family to pass the small plates to when he was close to death, so he gave care of them to King Benjamin.

 "King Benjamin was a holy man, and he did reign over his people in righteousness; . . . laboring with all the might of his body and the faculty of his whole soul" (Words of Mormon 1:17–18).

Reign in Righteousness (Mosiah 2–5)

When King Benjamin called his people together so he could share his final teachings and declare his son the new king, so many people showed up that there was not enough room for everyone. In his powerful speech about the life of the Savior and gratitude for the Savior's Atonement, King Benjamin pleaded with the people to take Christ's name and live like Him their whole lives. The people loved and respected King Benjamin because he had lived according to the things he taught.

"If I, whom ye call your king, who has spent his days in your service, and yet has been in the service of God, do merit any thanks from you, O how ye ought to thank your heavenly King!" (Mosiah 2:19)

King Benjamin spent all of his days protecting, serving, and leading his people to do good. He did not raise taxes and give himself a rich lifestyle; rather he worked alongside the people as their equal to care for the poor and needy. King Benjamin never put himself above anyone else. He gave his whole heart and soul for his people.

King Benjamin was a powerful leader, friend, father, and prophet because he tried to live like Christ.

? Will you follow King Benjamin's example and live as the Savior would in all places and with all people? Will you strive to develop Christlike attributes?

Activity

As a family, make a list of characteristics of Jesus Christ. Go through the list and invite family members to identify someone who is a good example of each characteristic. This could be a person from the scriptures or somebody they know. After your discussion, encourage everyone to set a goal to improve on one of these qualities. (For a list of Christlike attributes, see Chapter 7 of *Preach My Gospel*.)

King Mosiah II

King Mosiah II was a Nephite king who ruled over the people of Nephi in the land of Zarahemla. His father was King Benjamin, and he was probably named after his grandfather, King Mosiah I. Mosiah II was a righteous man and a respected leader of the Nephites. During his time as king, he sent one of his soldiers, named Ammon, to find a group of people who left the land of Zarahemla years before. Ammon was successful in finding the group and bringing them back with him. King Mosiah II was the last king of the Nephite nation. After him, the presiding government switched from kings to a group of judges.

 None of King Mosiah II's sons wanted to serve as king after their father. They wanted to preach the gospel instead.

 The sons of Mosiah II were Ammon, Aaron, Omner, and Himni. Along with Alma the Younger, they were rebellious and fought against the Church until they were converted to the Lord and became powerful missionaries.

 King Mosiah II was chosen to be king by his father around 124 BC. He served as king for thirty-three years.

 When King Mosiah II changed the government from a system of kings to judges, he appointed Alma the Younger as chief judge. He also gave Alma permission to establish the Church throughout the land.

 "And [the people] did wax strong in love towards Mosiah; yea, they did esteem him more than any other man; for they did not look upon him as a tyrant . . . , but he had established peace" (Mosiah 29:40).

The Gifts of the King (Mosiah 8, 28)

When Ammon returned with the people of Limhi—the group who had left the land of Zarahemla many years before—they brought with them a collection of gold plates they had found during their time away. The gold plates were written in a different language, and no one among their people could read them. When Ammon learned of the plates, he told the people of Limhi that the king, Mosiah II, was blessed by God with the gift to translate and would be able to reveal the truths the plates contained. He also testified that King Mosiah II had the gifts of prophecy and seership.

"Thus God has provided a means that man, through faith, might work mighty miracles; therefore he becometh a great benefit to his fellow beings." (Mosiah 8:18)

King Mosiah's spiritual gifts helped his people and many future generations to be blessed with great truths and come closer to Christ. Mosiah used his gifts for the benefit of others around him.

Our Heavenly Father has given each of us unique gifts, talents, and abilities. Our gifts may be different, but each was given to us so we could better bless and help our families, the Church, and all of Heavenly Father's children.

? What gifts and talents do you feel Heavenly Father has given you? How will you use your spiritual gifts to help the people in your family, school, neighborhood, or church live happier lives?

Activity

Give each person in your family a piece of paper, and have each one write his or her name at the top. Pass the papers around the family and ask everyone to write or draw a spiritual gift or talent they see in the person whose name is on the paper. After all family members have written on each of the papers, read them together and talk about how these gifts can be used to bless others.

Ammon

Ammon was a strong man who was trusted by King Mosiah II. A few years after Mosiah II was made king, his people started to ask about the people of Limhi, a group who had left the land of Zarahemla to return to the land they had come from. King Mosiah decided to send men to search for the group, and he selected Ammon to lead the search party. Ammon was successful in finding the people of Limhi, and after he heard their stories, he was able to help them return to the land of Zarahemla once they escaped from slavery. Even though he was a very powerful man, Ammon remained a humble servant of the king and of the Lord.

 This Ammon is not the same Ammon who was the son of King Mosiah II and went on a mission to the Lamanites.

 Ammon is a descendant of Zarahemla, the leader of the Mulekites who King Mosiah I met when his people left the land of Nephi.

 Ammon's search for the people of Limhi started around 121 BC.

 Ammon led a group of twenty-four men on the expedition to find the people of Limhi.

 "And it came to pass on the morrow they started to go up, having with them one Ammon, he being a strong and mighty man, . . . and he was also their leader" (Mosiah 7:3).

The Rescue Party (Mosiah 7,22)

The people of King Limhi had left the land of Zarahemla many years before Ammon arrived there with the Nephites. After much persuasion from the people, King Mosiah II sent Ammon with twenty-four men to find those who had left. The search party spent forty days wandering in the wilderness before they found the people of Limhi in bondage to the Lamanites. When the people of Limhi learned who Ammon and his men were, they rejoiced.

"And now, I will rejoice; and on the morrow I will cause that my people shall rejoice also. . . . Behold, our brethren will deliver us out of our bondage." (Mosiah 7:14–15)

Ammon and his men endured a difficult journey to find the lost people of Limhi. They traveled far and faced many hard days. It was also very difficult to arrange the people's escape from the Lamanites, but Ammon was ready and willing to take on the challenge. When they all returned to the city of Zarahemla, the people there rejoiced to learn that their lost brothers had been safely found.

Sometimes people get themselves into trouble that they cannot get out of by themselves. They may feel like they will never find peace and safety again. However, when those who are in trouble earnestly seek the Lord, Heavenly Father always sends an "Ammon" to rescue them. Sometimes you will be like the people of Limhi, needing rescue, and sometimes the Lord will send you as an Ammon—the rescuer.

? Will you be like Ammon and search out those who are lost and need your help spiritually?

Activity

Hide several items (coins, pieces of paper, buttons, etc.) somewhere in a room or throughout the house. Ask family members to search for one of these lost items and bring it back to a selected home base. When they do, they receive a treat or prize. Explain that we all have a responsibility to search out those who are lost. It may be difficult, but it is worth it!

Zeniff

During the reign of King Mosiah I, a man named Zeniff led a group of Nephites away from Zarahemla and back to the land of Nephi. He attempted this journey twice. The first try ended in a big fight among those traveling in the group. After the fight, Zeniff went back to Zarahemla, but later he decided to try the journey again. He and his followers moved into Lamanite territory and made a treaty with the king of the Lamanites to share their lands. For many years this Nephite colony was peaceful and successful. The people built many buildings and created a beautiful city. When Zeniff died, he passed the crown to his son, Noah, who became a wicked king.

 The first group to leave Zarahemla with Zeniff wanted to battle the Lamanites and take back their old lands. Zeniff refused to follow this plan.

 Zeniff's group left Zarahemla for the first time around 200 BC.

 For twenty-two years, Zeniff's people primarily lived in peace and prosperity within the land of Nephi.

 Laman, the king of the Lamanites, made a treaty with Zeniff hoping to enslave his people. Although the Lamanites attacked Zeniff's people, they were not enslaved until the reign of King Limhi, Zeniff's grandson.

 "And yet, I being over-zealous to inherit the land of our fathers, . . . started again on our journey into the wilderness to go up to the land; but we were smitten with famine and sore afflictions; for we were slow to remember the Lord our God" (Mosiah 9:3).

Foolish Desires (Mosiah 7–9)

During the time of King Mosiah I, the Lord warned His people to leave their land. They had lived there many years, but the Lord knew they would be safer and better off somewhere else. Not long after this, Zeniff and his group decided they wanted to return to the land they had come from. When they arrived, Zeniff saw good in the Lamanites who were there, and he decided to make a treaty with them and live as neighbors. He did not know that the Lamanite king had different plans.

"Zeniff, . . . he being over-zealous to inherit the land of his fathers, therefore being deceived by the cunning and craftiness of king Laman." (Mosiah 7:21)

Zeniff's decision to return to the land of Nephi led to great sorrow and hard times for his people. Even his grandson Limhi suffered from Zeniff's foolish decision. The king was not a wicked man, but he chose to rely on his own wisdom and ended up paying the consequences.

Sometimes we may act a little like Zeniff. We hear the warnings and counsel of the Lord, but when we want something different, we find reasons to believe we will be fine doing things our own way.

? Will you learn from Zeniff's example and always trust in the counsel of the Lord? Will you choose to follow and obey even when you think another way is better?

Activity

Have a family discussion about the standards in the *For the Strength of Youth* pamphlet. Talk about the excuses people might make for not following these standards. Read and emphasize the blessings promised to those who do uphold the Lord's standards.

King Noah

King Noah was a ruler of a group of people who broke off from the rest of the Nephites. Noah took over as king when his father, Zeniff, became too old to rule. When Noah was in power he changed everything good his father had established. He got rid of his father's righteous priests and chose his friends to rule with him, built large, expensive buildings and a palace for himself, spent money on vineyards for wine, and turned his kingdom into a wicked city. The Lord sent the prophet Abinadi to preach repentance to Noah and his people. Noah and his priests rejected Abinadi's message and burned him at the stake. The Lamanites eventually attacked the city, and Noah was burned by his own people, as Abinadi had prophesied.

 Noah began to rule in about 160 BC and died around 148 BC.

 Noah taxed the people under his rule twenty percent of everything they owned. These taxes paid for Noah's luxurious lifestyle.

 Alma the Elder was one of the priests in King Noah's court. He was converted by Abinadi's testimony and escaped the city.

 One of Noah's building projects was a large tower used to watch for invading Lamanites.

 Zeniff was Noah's father and had been a righteous leader, but Noah chose to be wicked.

 "Now the eyes of the people were blinded; therefore they hardened their hearts. . . . And king Noah hardened his heart against the word of the Lord, and he did not repent of his evil doings" (Mosiah 11:29).

Choose Carefully (Mosiah 11–12, 17)

King Noah was lazy, rude, and greedy. When the prophet Abinadi came to warn Noah's people that their wickedness would lead to destruction, Noah put him in jail.

Abinadi spoke against Noah's sins, and Noah felt guilty. He had been taught when he was young to be righteous, and he knew that Abinadi spoke the truth. Even though the words of the prophet struck Noah to the heart, he still condemned Abinadi to death.

"Now when king Noah had heard of the words which Abinadi had spoken unto the people, he was also wroth." (Mosiah 11:27)

After Abinadi's final warning, Noah was frightened and was about to let Abinadi go. However, the wicked priests reminded Noah of how awful Abinadi had made him feel. They told Noah that Abinadi should be punished for accusing the king of being wicked. When Noah heard the priests' words, he became angry again and ordered Abinadi's execution. Noah had surrounded himself with bad people, and they influenced him to make bad decisions. Noah gave in even when he knew it was wrong. Because of this, Noah eventually lost his life the same way he had killed Abinadi.

Other people can have a powerful influence on our decisions. Our choices have lasting consequences, so we need to be careful about whose counsel we follow when making important decisions.

? Do your friends convince you to ignore the prophets and make bad choices like Noah's priests did? Or do they make it easier for you to choose the right and live the gospel?

Activity

Have everyone write a thank-you note to a friend or family member who has made it easier for them to make righteous choices. They could thank the person they choose for his or her example and for influencing them to make good choices.

Abinadi

The prophet Abinadi was a powerful servant of Jesus Christ who was not afraid to teach the word of the Lord. Abinadi was called by the Lord to call the wicked King Noah and his people to repentance. King Noah's people kicked Abinadi out of the city and told him to never return. Two years later, the Lord sent Abinadi back to the city to preach repentance once again. The people captured Abinadi and delivered him to King Noah and his wicked priests. In the king's court the priests tried to trick Abinadi, but he delivered a powerful lesson about the Savior and repentance. In anger, Noah and his priests put Abinadi to death by fire.

 Abinadi preached to the people of King Noah around 150 BC.

 Many people think of Abinadi as an old man when he was preaching, but the scriptures do not actually tell us how old he was.

 Abinadi was the first martyr for Christ mentioned in the Book of Mormon. A martyr is someone who dies for what they believe in.

 There was only one person in Noah's court who believed Abinadi's testimony. That person was Alma the Elder, who escaped after hearing Abinadi teach about Christ.

 "And now, when Abinadi had said these words, he fell, having suffered death by fire; yea, having been put to death because he would not deny the commandments of God, having sealed the truth of his words by his death" (Mosiah 17:20).

Even Until Death (Mosiah 11–17)

The first time Abinadi came into the city to preach, the people rejected him and threatened his life. Abinadi must have feared for his life when the Lord commanded him to return to the city, but still he followed the Lord's command. Abinadi stood with courage and power and did not back down from the truth even when he was outnumbered. After preaching to King Noah, Abinadi was bound again and cast into prison. They told Abinadi they would not kill him if he would take back the things he had said. Abinadi would not.

"Yea, and I will suffer even until death, and I will not recall my words." (Mosiah 17:10)

Abinadi gave his life for Jesus Christ. Being a true and faithful servant of the Lord was more important to him than anything else.

You will probably not be asked to die for Jesus Christ, but each of us will have to sacrifice or go through difficult trials to stay faithful to Him.

? Would you be willing to give your life for Jesus Christ? Will you be courageous and sacrifice whatever you must in order to show your love for Him?

Activity

As a family, watch the film *Joseph Smith: The Prophet of the Restoration* for another example of someone who both lived and died for his testimony of Jesus Christ. You can find the film online on the Mormon Channel (mormonchannel.org).

Alma the Elder

Nephite

Alma the Elder was a powerful prophet, leader, and teacher among the Nephites. Before he was a great leader in the Church, Alma was a priest in King Noah's court. He lived a wicked lifestyle with the king and the other priests. Alma's heart changed when he heard the testimony of the prophet Abinadi. He escaped from King Noah's guards and led a group of people out of the city to start a new colony of faithful disciples. Unfortunately, the group later became slaves to the Lamanites. The Lord eventually delivered the people of Alma out of slavery, and they joined with the Nephites who were living in the land of Zarahemla. Alma faithfully served the Lord until he died.

 This Alma is called "Alma the Elder" because his son of the same name is also a significant person in the Book of Mormon. Alma the Younger was rebellious against the Church until he experienced a great change of heart.

 Alma the Elder was born around 173 BC. He was a descendant of Nephi, son of Lehi.

 Alma secretly taught and baptized people in the wilderness away from the city. The place where they were baptized was called the Waters of Mormon.

 After escaping from King Noah's court, Alma spent many days writing down Abinadi's testimony so future generations could learn from it.

 "And now, as ye are desirous to come into the fold of God, and to be called his people, and are willing to bear one another's burdens, that they may be light; Yea, and are willing to mourn with those that mourn; yea, and comfort those that stand in need of comfort, and to stand as witnesses of God at all times and in all things, and in all places that ye may be in" (Mosiah 18:8–9).

But There Was One (Mosiah 16–18)

When the prophet Abinadi was brought to King Noah's court in chains, Alma the Elder was one of the wicked priests there fighting against him. As Abinadi bore powerful testimony of the Savior, the Spirit touched Alma's heart. After Abinadi finished giving his testimony, King Noah commanded that his priests should take him away to be put to death. Perhaps Abinadi thought that his testimony had not been helpful and that his mission had been a failure.

"But there was one among them whose name was Alma, . . . and he believed the words which Abinadi had spoken." (Mosiah 17:2)

After Noah condemned Abinadi, Alma the Elder stood up to defend the prophet. He was chased out of the courts, and guards were sent to kill him. Alma spent the rest of his life preaching and teaching the gospel, establishing churches, and baptizing disciples of Christ. Abinadi probably had no idea the far-reaching influence his testimony would have as Alma the Elder taught his son Alma, who then taught his son Helaman, who taught his son Helaman, followed by his son Nephi, and then his son Nephi, who was the prophet living when Jesus Christ visited the people in America. Each of these men who became great prophets and powerful witnesses of Christ was blessed because of Abinadi's example and teachings. One righteous man's influence helped to bring about generations of righteousness.

You will have opportunities to do good, to keep your covenants, and to share your testimony and example with others. You may never know how many people your simple acts of righteousness will help.

? Will you continue to keep your covenants and share your testimony wherever you go? You really can change the world!

Activity

Set up a long row of dominoes standing upright. Choose someone to knock over the first domino, and watch what happens as it knocks the domino next to it. Discuss the impact that one small act of righteousness can have for generations to come. Perhaps you could share a picture or story of someone in your family history who made a righteous choice or joined the Church and then identify all the good that has come from his or her actions.

Limhi

PEOPLE OF **Zeniff**

King Limhi inherited a major problem when he became king of his small Nephite colony. Limhi was the son of King Noah and the grandson of King Zeniff. His people lived in the Land of Nephi as slaves to the Lamanites. Fortunately, Mosiah II, king in the land of Zarahemla, sent a search party to the land where King Limhi and his people were enslaved. This group of men helped deliver Limhi's people from slavery and took them back to the land of Zarahemla. Unlike his father, Limhi was a righteous king who tried to follow the commandments of the Lord. His righteousness was a great blessing to his people.

 In about 148 BC Limhi became the third king in the line of kings in his Nephite city.

 Limhi sent out a search party to find the land of Zarahemla before Ammon found him and his people. The search had been unsuccessful, but the group did find the remains of the Jaredite civilization and twenty-four gold plates that contained a record of their story.

 The people of Limhi were slaves to the Lamanites and had to give them half of everything they owned, made, or grew.

 Sometime after Limhi arrived in Zarahemla, he was taught and baptized by Alma, who was formerly one of his father's wicked priests but had been converted to the Lord.

 "But if ye will turn to the Lord with full purpose of heart, and put your trust in him, and serve him with all diligence of mind, if ye do this, he will, according to his own will and pleasure, deliver you out of bondage" (Mosiah 7:33).

Back on Track (Mosiah 21)

Limhi's father, King Noah, was a bad example to his son and brought a lot of wickedness into his kingdom. Noah was eventually chased out of the city and burned, and Limhi must have been very sad to see his father ruin his own happiness and the happiness of his people. The Lamanites became these Nephites' masters and killed many of Limhi's friends and family members. Limhi and his people had to work hard to pay taxes to the Lamanites. Noah had been very wicked and had left the kingdom with problems, but Limhi wanted to be different.

"They were desirous to be baptized as a witness and a testimony that they were willing to serve God with all their hearts." (Mosiah 21:35)

Sometimes problems come into our lives because of the bad choices of other people. We may sometimes see bad examples from family members or friends. However, we don't have to follow those examples. We can make the future better for ourselves and others by making good choices.

? Will you choose to live differently than any bad examples you may see? Will you serve the Lord even when you face trials that others have brought into your life?

Activity

Have everyone in the family except for one person sing a song together. Ask that person to try to sing a different song while the rest of the family sings together. Explain that it is hard to be the one person doing something different and standing alone—just like it is hard to do something right when so many others are doing wrong. Discuss how to be strong and stand for the right even when others do not.

Gideon

Nephite

Gideon was a faithful and courageous military leader who helped the Nephites in several situations. He was a soldier who became a man of great faith, living his life defending the gospel. When Ammon found the people of Limhi, he worked with Gideon and King Limhi to help the people escape to the land of Zarahemla. When Gideon was an old man, he was killed by a man named Nehor, who fought against the Church. Gideon is one of the Book of Mormon's finest heroes.

 Gideon has the same name as another military hero found in the Book of Judges in the Old Testament.

 After King Noah's death, Gideon became a trusted soldier of Noah's righteous son, Limhi.

 Gideon was so respected that the Nephites named a land, a valley, and a city after him.

 "And [Nehor] began to contend with him sharply, that he might lead away the people of the church; but [Gideon] withstood him, admonishing him with the words of God" (Alma 1:7).

Show Me Your Courage (Mosiah 19, 22, Alma 1)

Gideon was the kind of man that everyone wanted on his or her side. Gideon realized how wicked the king was and became angry. Gideon stood up to him for ruling unrighteously and putting the people of the city in great danger. He defended the people of the kingdom against Noah. Later, when the people were enslaved by the Lamanites, the brave Gideon approached the new king with a plan for escape—again standing up for his people.

"And now O king, if thou hast not found me to be an unprofitable servant, . . . I desire that thou woudst listen to my words at this time, and I will be thy servant and deliver this people out of bondage." (Mosiah 22:4)

When Gideon was an old man, the false teacher Nehor was trying to lead people away from the Church. Gideon knew this was wrong, and he courageously stood up to the man to protect the people of the city from his lies. Nehor attacked and killed Gideon with his sword.

Today, there are many people who lie and take advantage of others. The world needs people like Gideon to stand up courageously for those who need help.

? Will you be like Gideon and stand up for others when they need your help? Will you be brave and defend those who have a hard time defending themselves?

Activity

In your family, plan and act out a few skits depicting someone bravely standing up for someone else. You could create scenarios that take place at school, on the playground, at work, or anywhere else. After you perform the skits, talk about Christ and how He always took care of those in need.

Alma the Younger

Nephite

Alma the Younger is the son of Alma the Elder, a good father who was a priest in the courts of wicked King Noah. Alma the Younger was friends with the sons of King Mosiah, and they spent years rebelling against their parents and the Church. This group of young men eventually experienced a change of heart, repented, and became great leaders in the Church. Alma the Younger became the high priest over the whole Church and spent many years teaching the gospel and bringing thousands of people into the gospel. Many of his years were spent teaching with a companion named Amulek. Alma's teachings and missions make up a large part of the Book of Mormon.

 When the sons of Mosiah left for their missions to the Lamanites, Alma stayed to serve as high priest of the Church.

 Alma was appointed high priest of the Church in approximately 92 BC.

 Alma served as both the chief judge (like the president) and high priest (like the prophet) among the Nephites for some time, but he gave up the role of chief judge to focus on helping the Church.

 Mormon tells us that Alma left his people one day and was never heard of again. Many think he was either buried by the Lord or taken up to heaven like Moses was.

 "Now, as my mind caught hold upon this thought, I cried within my heart: O Jesus, . . . have mercy on me. . . . And now, behold, when I thought this, I could remember my pains no more" (Alma 36:18–19).

A God of Second Chances (Mosiah 27)

Even though he had been taught better, Alma made a lot of wrong choices. He spent his days in wickedness trying to convince other people to stop believing in God. He made fun of people who were righteous.

One day, the Lord sent an angel to Alma to tell him that he was in great spiritual danger and needed to repent. Alma spent three days feeling horrible. He thought about all the wrong he had done. He thought that God would never want to forgive him. Right when he felt there was no hope for him, he remembered what his father had taught him about Jesus Christ. He remembered that the Savior provided God's children with second chances and that Heavenly Father would forgive people who wanted to change.

"And oh, what joy, and what marvelous light I did behold; yea, my soul was filled with joy as exceeding as was my pain!" (Alma 36:20)

Alma decided to change his life. He made things right with his parents and everyone he had hurt. He spent the rest of his life teaching people about the Savior.

Everyone makes mistakes in their lives. Sometimes people we know walk away from Heavenly Father and His Church. But just like Alma the Younger, we believe in a God of second chances. He loves us and is willing to forgive anyone who decides they want to change and come back to Him.

? Will you love and help others even when they make mistakes? Will you turn to the Lord and try to change when you make mistakes in your life?

Activity

Print out or draw a maze. Let everyone try to draw a path through the whole maze without lifting the pencil or making any mistakes. If someone makes a mistake, say that he or she can start over and try again. No matter how many attempts it takes, everyone who finishes the maze then gets the same reward.

Book of Alma

Nehor

Nephite

Nehor was a wicked man who caused a lot of trouble among the Nephites. He lived in the land of Zarahemla during the reign of the judges and decided to start his own religion and fight against the true Church of God. Nehor taught lies and spread his false religion to as many people as he could. The scriptures say he was a large and strong man who pretended to be a prophet. Gideon, who also lived in Zarahemla, stood up to Nehor and tried to help the people see through his lies. This made Nehor angry, and he killed Gideon with a sword. Nehor was put to death for his crimes, but many people continued to believe the lies he taught.

 Nehor was the first person to introduce priestcraft in Zarahemla. Priestcraft is the teaching of false doctrines or trying to become a religious leader in order to be popular or rich.

 Gideon was the brave soldier who had helped deliver the Nephites from the Lamanites. Nehor's murder of Gideon brought much sadness.

 Nehor's false religion was called "the order of Nehor."

 Many people followed the false teachings of Nehor in the city of Ammonihah. The city was destroyed in 81 BC, and the place came to be called "the Desolation of Nehors."

 "And it came to pass that he did teach these things so much that many did believe on his words, even so many that they began to support him and give him money. And he began to be lifted up in the pride of his heart" (Alma 1:5–6).

Choose Wisely (Alma 1)

Nehor was a very persuasive and popular speaker. He was bold and charismatic, and the people loved his lies. He taught people they could do whatever they wanted and Heavenly Father would not care. According to Nehor, they could lie, steal, and hurt others and there would be no punishments.

"And he also testified unto the people that all mankind should be saved at the last day, and that they need not fear nor tremble." (Alma 1:4)

Nehor had a lot of friends, but what he was doing was wrong. The people who listened to him and followed him were guilty of many wicked things, and they suffered because of it.

There are people in the world who will try to get you to turn away from Jesus Christ and His Church. They will tell you lies and other things to try to convince you to lower your standards. They will tell you it is more important to be rich and popular than it is to be good. Avoid these people. They can ruin you. The words of the scriptures that Gideon taught helped people avoid the lies of Nehor. They will also help you.

? Will you be careful to avoid the influence of people who try to turn you against the Lord? Will you stay close to the Lord so you can recognize evil when you are confronted with it?

Activity

Bake two batches of cookies that look the same. Put the right amount of sugar in one batch, and in the other replace the sugar with salt. Have everyone choose and taste a cookie from one of the batches. Talk about how some things may look appealing but will actually be bad for you and make you spiritually sick. Discuss as a family how to detect and avoid spiritual "salty cookies."

Amlici

Amlicite

Before King Mosiah II died, he changed the government of the Nephites from being ruled by a king to having a presiding set of judges. He thought that system would prevent dangerous kings like Noah from taking over again. Amlici was a wicked man who tried to change the government back and make himself king. He also wanted to destroy the Church of God. He gathered a lot of followers and called on the Nephites to vote on whether he should be king. When he lost the vote, he and his followers decided to wage a war against the rest of the Nephites. They were defeated, but Amlici joined a Lamanite army and returned to fight again. The army of Amlici destroyed many things on their way to Zarahemla and many people were killed, but the Nephites finally defeated the army, and Amlici died in battle.

 Amlici lived in Zarahemla around the year 87 BC.

 The people who followed Amlici were called Amlicites, and they were known for marking their foreheads to be different from the Nephites.

 Amlici was a member of the order of Nehor, the false religion that Nehor created to fight against the Church of God.

 In the great battle of the Nephite army and Amlici's army, Alma defeated Amlici in a one-on-one sword fight.

 "And in one year were thousands and tens of thousands of souls sent to the eternal world, that they might reap their rewards according to their works. . . . For every man receiveth wages of him whom he listeth to obey, and this according to the words of the spirit of prophecy" (Alma 3:26–27).

Marked (Alma 2–3)

Amlici decided at some point in his life that he did not want to follow the commandments or live righteously. He wanted power and money and popularity more than he wanted truth and faith, so he decided to rebel against the Lord. There were many people who joined with Amlici in rebelling against what was right and true. This group of people did not want to be like the rest of the Nephites, so they marked their foreheads with a red marking to show that they were not part of the Church.

"Now the Amlicites knew not that they were fulfilling the words of God when they began to mark themselves in their foreheads; nevertheless they had come out in open rebellion against God." (Alma 3:18)

Anyone who saw the Amlicites knew that they loved worldly things more than they loved God. That is the message they chose to send to everyone.

Each of us sends a message to the people around us. The things we wear, the way we talk, the music we listen to, the pictures on our wall, and the movies we like all signal to other people what we care about in our hearts. We should not judge another person based on what we see on the outside, but we should be careful not to mark ourselves in rebellion against God.

? What message do your choices, words, and actions send? What can you do to make sure that when others see or hear you they know you are a follower of Jesus Christ?

Activity

Have everyone find an item that demonstrates that they are a follower of Jesus Christ. It could be a picture, a set of scriptures, a modest outfit, a CTR ring, or another item. Once everyone has found their item, gather together and have everyone share what they found and what that item tells other people about them.

Amulek

Ammonihahite

Amulek was a righteous Nephite who served for many years as one of the most powerful missionaries of the Book of Mormon. When he was younger, Amulek was a wealthy and well-known citizen of the city of Ammonihah, but he was not a very active member of the Church. One day, an angel visited him in a dream and asked him to feed a prophet of God who was coming to the city. This prophet was Alma the Younger, and his visit changed Amulek's life. Alma and Amulek became missionary companions and spent many years together preaching the gospel. They faced many hardships during the years they were preaching, including being tortured and thrown in prison. However, they also witnessed many miracles and helped people change during their time as missionaries. Some of the great chapters in the Book of Mormon about Jesus Christ are records from Amulek's teachings.

 Alma the Younger and Amulek spent about eight years together as missionaries.

 Amulek was a descendant of Nephi, son of Lehi.

 One of the success stories of Amulek's mission is the conversion of Zeezrom—a lawyer who once fought against Amulek and then later joined him as a fellow missionary.

 Amulek sacrificed his family, friends, home, and great wealth to become a missionary and faithful member of Christ's Church.

 "And as many as would hear their words, unto them they did impart the word of God, without any respect of persons, continually. And thus did Alma and Amulek go forth . . . to preach the word throughout all the land" (Alma 16:14–15).

The Hand of the Lord (Alma 8–10)

The city where Amulek lived was very wicked. The people there rejected the words of the scriptures and the prophets. Alma was kicked out of the city for preaching the gospel, but the Lord told him to return and try again. When he returned, he met Amulek. Amulek took Alma to his home, where he fed and cared for him. Amulek's heart was touched by the words of Alma, and he began to recognize his blessings. He realized that for many years he had ignored the hand of the Lord in his life and the great privileges of living the gospel. The Lord had reached out to him many times, but he had been too busy to notice.

"For I have seen much of his mysteries and his marvelous power; . . . Nevertheless, I did harden my heart, for I was called many times and I would not hear; therefore I knew concerning these things, yet I would not know." (Alma 10:5–6)

Once Amulek opened his heart, he started to recognize what Heavenly Father had done for him. His gratitude helped him learn more things of the Spirit.

Our Heavenly Father and Jesus Christ are constantly blessing us and providing us with tender mercies. Like Amulek, we may sometimes have ungrateful hearts or fail to recognize the hand of the Lord in our lives.

? Will you watch for the ways that Heavenly Father blesses you every day? Will you thank Him often for how good He is to you?

Activity

Find a notebook or journal for your family to use to count your blessings. For at least a week, have everyone write in the journal the blessings from Heavenly Father they notice. Gather after the week to read and share everyone's experiences. Invite your family to continue adding to the blessing journal.

Zeezrom

Ammonihahite

The city of Ammonihah was a very wicked place with corrupt judges and lawyers. Zeezrom was one of these lawyers, and he tried to turn the people of the city against the prophet Alma and his missionary companion, Amulek. Zeezrom told Amulek that he would pay him a great deal of money to tell the people there was no God. Instead, Amulek and Alma were able to teach Zeezrom and others with him about Jesus Christ. The teachings deeply affected Zeezrom, who started to feel guilty for his sins and the bad decisions he was making. Zeezrom later became a wonderful missionary and did a lot of good in the Church.

 Zeezrom was a legal official in the city of Ammonihah around 82 BC.

 Though he originally tried to trick the missionaries, Zeezrom was converted and became a great missionary for the Lord.

 Zeezrom told Amulek he would pay him six onties if he would deny God—that is about forty-two days' worth of pay.

 Alma miraculously healed Zeezrom from a terrible sickness—even after Zeezrom turned the people of Ammonihah against him.

 "And they went in unto the house unto Zeezrom; and they found upon his bed, sick, being very low with a burning fever; and his mind also was exceedingly sore because of his iniquities; and when he saw them he stretched forth his hand, and besought them that they would heal him" (Alma 15:5).

From That Time Forth (Alma 11–15)

Zeezrom was caught up doing the same bad things as everyone else in his city. He was selfish, told lies, and made a lot of money starting fights. The day he tried to trick Alma and Amulek turned into an important day for Zeezrom's eternal welfare. When the missionaries answered his questions, Zeezrom began to feel the truth of what they were saying. When he heard their testimony, he believed them. Zeezrom had gathered a crowd of people to watch him ruin Alma and Amulek's mission, but he changed his mind once he knew he was wrong.

"And it came to pass that [Zeezrom] began to cry unto the people, saying: Behold, I am guilty, and these men are spotless before God. And he began to plead for them from that time forth." (Alma 14:7)

The people kicked Zeezrom out of the city for defending Alma and Amulek. It must have been very hard for Zeezrom to turn his life around, but once he knew the truth, he acted on it immediately.

Sometimes we find that we are living in a way that is not right or that some of our actions are not what the Lord wants of us. We can be like Zeezrom and turn around immediately once we recognize that we are headed in the wrong direction.

? Will you make changes when you feel that you are doing something wrong? Will you make those changes immediately—no matter what you may have to sacrifice?

Activity

Visit the Mormon Channel online and watch the Mormon Message from Elder Jeffrey R. Holland called "Wrong Roads." After your family watches it, discuss what Elder Holland's story teaches. How is the Elder Holland's experience similar to Zeezrom's? How is it different?

Ammon

 **NePhite**

Ammon the missionary was one of the four sons of the Nephite king Mosiah II. In his earlier years, Ammon, his brothers, and Alma the Younger fought against the Church and were rude and nasty to the members. They made a big change in their lives after they were visited by an angel of the Lord and told to repent. All four sons of Mosiah refused to be the king after their father stepped down. They decided that instead they wanted to spend the rest of their lives serving as missionaries and bringing people unto Christ. They served many missions and taught the gospel to many people. One of Ammon's most successful missions was to the land of the Lamanites, where he taught King Lamoni and his wife about the Savior. Thousands of people were converted and the Church grew much stronger because of Ammon's great work.

 Ammon's mission to the Lamanites lasted fourteen years. He was appointed as the head missionary among his brothers.

 Ammon is known for miraculously defending the flocks of King Lamoni against an invading group of Lamanites.

 King Lamoni's father was also brought into the Church after an encounter with Ammon.

 The people Ammon served in the Lamanite lands changed their name to reflect their conversion. They became known as the people of Ammon or the Anti-Nephi-Lehies.

 "Ammon said unto him: I am a man; and man in the beginning was created after the image of God, and I am called by his Holy Spirit to teach these things unto this people, that they may be brought to a knowledge of that which is just and true" (Alma 18:34).`

Prepare the Chariots (Alma 17-18)

When Ammon and his brothers went on a mission to the land of the Lamanites, they knew that they were going among a rebellious and angry people. Very soon after Ammon stepped into King Lamoni's lands, he was tied up, threatened, and brought to stand before the king. Ammon explained that all he wanted to do was become a servant of King Lamoni. When Lamoni gave Ammon the job of guarding his flocks from thieves, Ammon risked his life to serve the king and defend the flock. When the other servants returned to tell the king about Ammon's loyalty and bravery, Lamoni was surprised and touched. After defending the king's flocks, Ammon went to the stables to prepare Lamoni's chariots for a journey.

"Now when king Lamoni heard that Ammon was preparing his horses and his chariots he was more astonished, because of the faithfulness of Ammon, saying: Surely there has not been any servant among all my servants that has been so faithful as this man." (Alma 18:10)

Ammon's service and faithfulness softened the king's heart. Lamoni wanted to know more about Ammon's faith and the gospel because of what he saw in Ammon's heart.

One of the best ways we can show others what we believe is through the way that we treat them. Before you can ever share what you believe with someone, you have to show that you care.

? Will you love other people and find ways to serve them faithfully?

Activity

Plan and carry out a service project together as a family. Try to think of a way you can serve someone above and beyond what you would normally do. Perhaps you can invite another family to join in the service project with you.

King Lamoni

Ishmaelite

King Lamoni ruled a small kingdom with his wife in the land of Nephi. Other members of his family lived in nearby kingdoms and were rulers as well. Many of Lamoni's servants were afraid of the king because he would put them to death if they failed in their responsibilities. Lamoni, his wife, and his people were eventually taught the gospel by Ammon, a Nephite missionary who was one of the sons of King Mosiah. This group of people changed their lives and joined Christ's Church.

 King Lamoni lived and ruled around 90 BC.

 Lamoni offered one of his daughters to Ammon to marry, but Ammon declined, choosing to focus on serving the king and the Lord.

 The stripling warriors are some of the sons of Lamoni's people.

 After their conversion, Lamoni's people adopted the name of Anti-Nephi-Lehies, which most likely means they wanted to be like Nephi and Lehi.

 "I have seen my Redeemer . . . and he shall redeem all mankind who believe on his name. Now, when he had said these words, his heart was swollen within him, and he sunk again with joy; and the queen also sunk down, being overpowered by the Spirit" (Alma 19:13).

I Will Believe (Alma 18–19)

King Lamoni did not seem to be a kind or generous Lamanite leader. When Ammon showed up as a missionary in his land, Lamoni had him tied up and treated roughly. Lamoni had been taught to hate the Nephites and their religion.

Ammon offered to work as a servant of the king and miraculously defended the king's flocks. This surprised Lamoni, and he wondered where Ammon's power came from. Ammon taught King Lamoni that his strength came from God and that God had sent him with a message. King Lamoni started to trust Ammon and asked him to teach him about his God. Ammon told the king he would teach him only if he promised to listen. The king answered with faith.

"I will believe all thy words." (Alma 18:23)

King Lamoni and his wife were willing to believe and obey before Ammon ever spoke. Ammon taught them about Jesus Christ and His plan of salvation. The truths were so powerful that Lamoni, his wife, and his whole household fell to the ground and fainted with happiness and love for God.

The truth about Christ brought hope and happiness into Lamoni's life. This can happen to anyone who is willing to believe.

? Will you choose to believe the words and testimony of God's servants? Will you be like Lamoni and his wife and choose to believe and follow the truth?

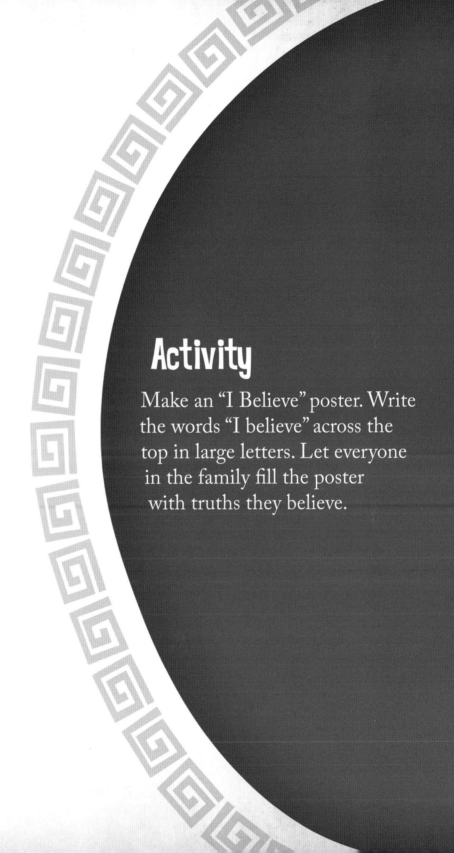

Activity

Make an "I Believe" poster. Write the words "I believe" across the top in large letters. Let everyone in the family fill the poster with truths they believe.

Lamanite

Abish was a Lamanite woman who lived in the land of Ishmael as a servant to the queen—the wife of King Lamoni. Abish was serving at the time that Ammon came from the land of Zarahemla to be a servant and missionary among her people. Abish already had a testimony of the gospel and was converted unto the Lord, but she kept it a secret from everyone. No one else in the king's land was a believer. When the king and queen were taught the gospel and converted to the Lord, Abish brought the people of the town together to witness the miracle. She was a great instrument in spreading the gospel among the people of the kingdom.

 Abish was converted to the Lord many years before Ammon came to her lands because of a vision her father had received.

 The conversion experience with Ammon, the king, the queen, and Abish happened around 90 BC.

 Abish recognized the Lord's hand in protecting Ammon from an angry Lamanite thief.

 When Abish brought people to the king's house to witness the conversion of the king and queen, many argued whether Ammon was from the devil or from God. Abish remained steadfast and faithful.

 "Thus, having been converted to the Lord, and never having made it known, therefore, when she saw that all the servants of Lamoni had fallen to the earth, and also her mistress, the queen, and the king, and Ammon lay prostrate on the earth, she knew that it was the power of God" (Alma 19:17).

Spread the News (Alma 19)

Abish kept her conversion to Jesus Christ a secret for many years. Perhaps she knew in her heart that it was best to wait for the right time for others to hear and receive the gospel. When Ammon, the king, the queen, and all of the household had such a powerful spiritual experience, Abish was very excited.

"And supposing that this opportunity, by making known unto the people what had happened . . . would cause them to believe in the power of God, therefore she ran forth from house to house, making it known unto the people." (Alma 19:17)

When Abish saw that there was an opportunity to share the gospel with others, she took it. She did not walk from house to house, but she ran. She wanted everyone she could find to know that Heavenly Father has great power and great love for His children. Abish was able to gather many people together through her diligence and enthusiasm. Many people came unto Christ because of the efforts of Abish.

We know the best truths in the history of the world. We have a knowledge of our Savior and of the restoration of His Church. Like Abish, we can find opportunities to bring the good news to anyone who will hear.

? Will you watch for opportunities to share your testimony and your love for the gospel of Jesus Christ? Will you be diligent like Abish and share the gospel with anyone and everyone who will listen?

Activity

Get a ball or a beanbag and have everyone sit in a circle. Throw the ball or beanbag around the circle. When a person catches it, have him or her say one thing about the gospel that brings happiness. See how long you can toss the ball without repeating anything. Afterward, talk about ways to seize opportunities to bring this happiness to others.

Aaron

Nephite

Aaron was one of the four sons of King Mosiah II. Along with Alma the Younger, Aaron and his brothers were rebellious and fought against the Church when they were young. A call to repentance from an angel of the Lord caused them to change. Aaron and his brothers decided they wanted to spend the rest of their lives preaching the gospel and helping other people. Aaron is a great missionary in the Book of Mormon. He went with his brothers on a mission to the Lamanites for many years. He had a very difficult mission but was an instrument in the hands of the Lord in bringing many thousands of people unto Christ and His Church.

 King Lamoni's father learned the gospel from Aaron after being impressed by Aaron's brother Ammon.

 Aaron tried to preach the gospel in at least three different Lamanite cities without any success.

 King Lamoni and Ammon came to the land of Middoni to free Aaron from prison.

 Alma the Younger and Aaron and his brothers reunited several years after their missions. It was a joyful meeting—especially because they were all still faithful in the gospel.

 "And it came to pass that they journeyed many days in the wilderness, and they fasted much and prayed much that the Lord would grant unto them a portion of his Spirit to go with them, and abide with them, that they might be an instrument in the hands of God" (Alma 17:9).

Brave Hearts (Alma 21–23)

The Lamanites were a wicked and ferocious people and hated the Nephites. Aaron and his brothers knew this, but when the Lord called them to serve a mission among the Lamanites, they went without delay. Aaron did not have much success at the beginning of his mission. He went to one city and was kicked out. In the next city he was mocked and rejected. When he went to a third city, he was tied up and thrown into prison without much food or water.

"Nevertheless they were patient in all their sufferings. And, as it happened, it was their lot to have fallen into the hands of a more hardened and a more stiffnecked people." (Alma 20:29–30)

Even though Aaron's experience was very difficult, he kept trying. When his brother Ammon helped him get out of prison, Aaron went on to the next city and continued to preach and serve. With the help of the Lord, Aaron faced his fears with bravery, suffered with patience, and accomplished hard things.

The Lord may ask us to do difficult things in our lives. There will be assignments and promptings that are scary or seem impossible. At these times we can remember the example of Aaron and face our challenges with faith that the Lord will strengthen us.

? Will you face your trials and challenges with bravery and faith? Will you pray for strength from the Lord to do the difficult things He asks you to do?

Activity

You probably know somebody who is currently serving a full-time mission for the Lord. He or she might be facing something hard or scary. As a family, write letters to encourage one or more missionaries to be brave, trust in the Lord, and do hard things.

King Lamoni's Father

Book of Alma

Ishmaelite

King Lamoni's father was the king over all of the Lamanite territories in the land of Nephi. As his son, King Lamoni ruled over part of the land with his wife. Ammon, a Nephite missionary, visited King Lamoni, taught him the gospel, and baptized him into the Church. While on their way to help Ammon's brother in another part of the land, Ammon and King Lamoni met King Lamoni's father. He was angry with Lamoni for spending time with a Nephite and told Lamoni to kill Ammon. When his son refused, Lamoni's father became angry and tried to kill Lamoni. Ammon risked his life to defend Lamoni. Lamoni's father was so touched by Ammon's love for his son that his heart was opened and he later joined the Church.

Aaron, the brother of Ammon, was prompted to visit Lamoni's father after his encounter with Ammon. Aaron then taught Lamoni's father the gospel.

After King Lamoni's father was converted to the Lord, he sent a proclamation throughout all the Lamanite kingdoms giving the Nephite missionaries freedom to preach wherever they wanted.

The people of King Lamoni and his father called themselves the Anti-Nephi-Lehies after they were converted. Their children included the young men who would become the stripling warriors.

King Lamoni's father reigned from about 90 BC to 77 BC. He died the year the converted Lamanites left the land of Nephi to join with the Nephites in the land of Zarahemla.

"And now it came to pass that when the king had sent forth this proclamation, that Aaron and his brethren went forth from city to city, and from one house of worship to another, . . . to preach and to teach the word of God among them; and thus they began to have great success. And thousands were brought to the knowledge of the Lord" (Alma 23:4–5).

More than Anything (Alma 20–23)

King Lamoni's father had a very deep hatred for the Nephites. When he met Ammon and Lamoni on the road, the old king attacked Lamoni. Ammon defended Lamoni against the attack, and Lamoni's father was very surprised. He thought Ammon would try to kill him, so he offered half of his kingdom to save his life. When Lamoni's father later met Aaron, Ammon's brother, he immediately wanted to hear about Aaron's beliefs. Aaron's testimony touched his heart.

"What shall I do that I may have this eternal life of which thou hast spoken? . . . I will give up all that I possess, yea, I will forsake my kingdom, that I may receive this great joy." (Alma 22:15)

King Lamoni's father was willing to do whatever it took to gain eternal life, even give up his kingdom. In his first prayer, King Lamoni's father promised that he would give up all of his sins to know God. He then did exactly that. He died a faithful servant of the Lord after doing much good.

Our Heavenly Father has great gifts, joys, and blessings available for us. His gifts are greater than anything the world can give us.

? What would you give up to know the Lord and receive His blessings? Would you sacrifice everything like King Lamoni's father did—including all of your sins—to receive eternal life?

Activity

Have everyone make a list of some memorable items they have bought or received as a gift. Next to these lists, make lists of blessings and gifts from Heavenly Father. Discuss which list is more valuable and why.

Anti-Nephi-Lehies

The Anti-Nephi-Lehies are a group of Lamanites who converted to the Lord and stayed faithful and strong their whole lives. This group of Lamanites had lived in the lands that were ruled over by King Lamoni's father. When King Lamoni and his father became believers, they encouraged the people in their lands to listen to the message of the missionaries. These Lamanite saints took this new name to show they were going to live a different, faithful life. When they converted, it made other Lamanites angry with them. To avoid problems, the Anti-Nephi-Lehies eventually moved into the land of Jershon and were watched over and protected by the Nephites.

 The Anti-Nephi-Lehies were also known as the "people of Ammon" or "Ammonites" because Ammon was the missionary who first brought them the gospel.

 The sons of the Anti-Nephi-Lehies were known as the two thousand stripling warriors.

 The Lamanite army that was angry about the Anti-Nephi-Lehies' conversion attacked the people, killing over a thousand of them. They did not fight back.

 The name "Anti-Nephi-Lehies" most likely means *of* or *like* Nephi and Lehi.

 "And as sure as the Lord liveth, so sure as many as believed, or as many as were brought to the knowledge of the truth, through the preaching of Ammon and his brethren, according to the spirit of revelation and of prophecy, and the power of God working miracles in them—yea, I say unto you, as the Lord liveth, as many of the Lamanites as believed in their preaching, and were coverted unto the Lord, never did fall away" (Alma 23:6).

Bury Them Deep (Alma 24–25)

The Anti-Nephi-Lehies did not live righteous lives before they were converted to the Lord. When they repented of their sins, they made a covenant with Heavenly Father that they would never return to their wicked ways ever again. In order to show the Lord how committed they were to their promises, the Anti-Nephi-Lehies took all of their swords and other weapons and buried them.

"They took their swords, and all the weapons . . . and they did bury them up deep in the earth. And this they did, it being in their view a testimony to God." (Alma 24:17–18)

One time, an army of the Anti-Nephi-Lehies' enemies attacked them, angry with them for converting. The Anti-Nephi-Lehies chose to die rather than break their covenant with the Lord not to shed blood. When their enemies saw this, many of them were touched and decided to change their own lives.

Each of us has made or will make covenants and promises with the Lord. Imagine how wonderful our lives would be if we kept those covenants with the same dedication that the Anti-Nephi-Lehies did. What if we decided today that we would never break our covenants?

? Are you willing to always keep your covenants to your Heavenly Father? What will you do to remove things from your life that would tempt you to break your covenants?

Activity

Cut out small pieces of paper in the shape of swords. Have everyone in the family write on a paper sword one thing that they feel might tempt them or keep them from upholding their covenants. Go outside and find a place where everyone can bury their paper swords, burying away those things that might get in the way of keeping their covenants.

Korihor

Nephite

Korihor was an evil man who came among the Nephites to convince them not to believe in Jesus Christ or the prophets. Korihor did not believe that people could know of things that would happen in the future. He taught that the prophets were just pretending to know about Jesus Christ in order to manipulate the people. Korihor went around to different parts of the land to spread these lies among the people. The Nephites were not sure what to do with him, so they sent him to Alma the Younger, the head of the Church. Korihor argued with Alma and demanded that he prove to him that God was real. Alma bore his testimony to him, but Korihor refused to believe.

 Korihor was called an anti-Christ in the Book of Mormon. An anti-Christ is anyone who fights against the Savior or His Church.

 Korihor went into the land of Jershon to spread his false teachings to the Anti-Nephi-Lehies, but they refused to listen to a single word. They tied him up and took him out of their city.

 Alma refused to ask for a sign to prove that God was real, but when Korihor insisted, the Lord struck Korihor dumb, meaning he could no longer speak.

 After Korihor was struck deaf and dumb, he had to beg for food to survive. He later died after being trampled by a crowd of people.

 "And thus we see the end of him who perverteth the ways of the Lord; and thus we see that the devil will not support his children at the last day, but doth speedily drag them down" (Alma 30:60).

The Not-So-Easy Way (Alma 30)

After he was struck down by the Lord, Korihor admitted that he had always known there was a God and that he had been lying. He told Alma that he was tricked by the devil to tell these lies to the people.

"I taught them because they were pleasing unto the carnal mind; and I taught them, even until I had much success." (Alma 30:53)

Korihor told lies that were pleasing to hear and easy to follow. He told people that there was no God, no sin, and that they could do whatever they wanted with no consequences. This made Korihor very popular. The people did not want to keep the commandments. They liked the sins they were committing, and they said their choices made them happy. In the end, it was not a better way to live. Korihor died a very lonely, sad, and unpopular person.

Always doing whatever you want may sound like a fun way to live. There are many people in the world who claim that you can do whatever you want and be happy. That is not true. Following the Lord's standards bring true happiness.

? Will you follow the standards and commandments of the Lord even when people say they don't matter?

Activity

As a family, go through the *For the Strength of Youth* booklet or brainstorm some of the commandments our Heavenly Father has given us. First talk about why some people might choose to break them. Then make a list of ways that following these commandments keeps you safe and blesses you.

Zoramites

The Zoramites were a group of Nephites who separated from the true Church of God to form their own religion in a land called Antionum. They knew the truth, but they decided not to follow it. They were led by a man named Zoram. He taught people to bow down to false idols instead of believing in Jesus Christ. Alma and some other missionaries went on a special mission to the land of Antionum to help the Zoramites repent and come back to the Church. Zoram and his people refused to listen to Alma and his companions. Alma and his companions were able to teach the poor, humble people who had been kicked out of the Zoramite church. Those who believed in Alma's teachings about Jesus Christ left the Zoramites and joined the people of Anti-Nephi-Lehi.

 A group of apostate Zoramites eventually joined with the Lamanites. Some of them later joined the Gadianton robbers—an evil group formed later that tried to destroy the Nephites.

 The Zoramites built a large tower called the Rameumptom. One by one the people of the church stood on top of it to recite a vain, memorized prayer.

 One of the missionaries who went with Alma to try to help the Zoramites was Zeezrom, the lawyer who had once fought against Alma.

 The Zoramites only allowed wealthy people into their church to worship, even though the poor people had helped build the church.

"They had fallen into great errors, for they would not observe to keep the commandments of God, . . . Neither would they observe the performances of the church, to continue in prayer and supplication to God daily, that they might not enter into temptation" (Alma 31:9–10).

Anything You Can Do I Can Do Better (Alma 31–32)

Alma and his missionary companions were disappointed by what they saw in the church of the Zoramites. The Zoramites had built a giant tower called the Rameumptom. A person stood on top of the tower and prayed about how lucky they were to be better than everyone else. They thanked Heavenly Father for helping them to become more holy. When they were done, the next person went up and said the exact same prayer. Alma cried and prayed for help.

"O, how long, O Lord, wilt thou suffer that thy servants shall dwell here . . . ? Behold, O God, they cry unto thee, and yet their hearts are swallowed up in their pride." (Alma 31:26–27)

The Zoramites thought they were better than the other people of their city because of the things that they had. They loved riches, fancy clothes, and other worldly things. Zoram taught his people that they were better because they had more treasures, so they treated poor people very badly.

Sometimes we might be tempted to think we are better than someone else because of the things we have. This is not true. God loves all of His children. We are never better or more important than anyone else in the world.

? Will you live in a way that shows that you do not think you are better than anyone? Will you be kind to everyone no matter how they dress, look, or act?

Activity

Have everyone in the family think of someone they know who is different than they are. Have each family member make a goal to perform one random act of service for that person in the coming week. It can be as simple as smiling and saying hello or leaving the person a kind note.

71

Chief Captain Moroni

Moroni was the head commander of the Nephite armies during one of the most war-filled times in the Book of Mormon. During Moroni's lifetime, the Lamanites were continually at war with the Nephites. One of his successful war strategies was to fortify and defend the Nephite cities by building up walls and digging ditches before the Lamanite armies attacked. He worked with the people to strengthen the weak parts of their cities and their lives. Captain Moroni did not want to go to war with the Lamanites, but when the Lamanite armies kept attacking, Moroni taught the people it was important to defend themselves and their families. There were many Nephite captains, but Moroni was the chief of the entire Nephite army.

 Moroni began fighting against the Lamanite armies around 74 BC.

 The Nephites appointed Moroni as chief captain when he was only twenty-five years old.

 The wars that Moroni fought in lasted for seventeen years.

 Chief Captain Moroni was not the same Moroni, son of Mormon, who buried the plates in the Hill Cumorah.

 "Yea, verily, verily I say unto you, if all men had been, and were, and ever would be, like unto Moroni, behold, the very powers of hell would have been shaken forever; yea, the devil would never have power over the hearts of the children of men" (Alma 48:17).

Defender of the Faith (Alma 46, 48)

Chief Captain Moroni was the head of the Nephite armies during a very dangerous time. Many of the Nephites were afraid of the Lamanite armies. The enemies were strong and fierce, and they were constantly threatening the Nephites' lives, families, and church. Captain Moroni gathered the Nephites together to convince them to fight the Lamanites. He stood up in front of them, tore his coat, and wrote a message on it. The message was called the Title of Liberty. These are the words he wrote:

"In memory of our God, our religion, and freedom, and our peace, our wives, and our children." (Alma 46:12)

Moroni knew that these were things worth fighting for. He was not going to let anyone take them away. Moroni was willing to give everything to defend what was right—even his own life. The Nephites rallied around him. Nothing was going to stop them from defending righteousness and the Church of God.

The enemy has not stopped fighting against family and faith. The Lord needs His servants to stand up for what is right.

? Will you stand for the truth wherever you go? Will you stand with Moroni, defending and supporting God, religion, freedom, and family?

Activity

Construct a Title of Liberty for your family. You can write it on a poster or a flag or piece of fabric, like Moroni's coat. Have your family members write on the Title of Liberty the values you embrace and want to defend as a family. Place it somewhere everyone can see it as a reminder.

Amalickiah and Ammoron

Amalickiahite

Amalickiah and Ammoron were two wicked Nephite brothers who spent some time as leaders over the Lamanite army. Amalickiah took advantage of people and made himself a leader of a group that fought against the Church. When Captain Moroni stopped him, he left the Nephites. He lied and murdered people until he became a leader of the Lamanite army and then eventually the king. After his death, his brother Ammoron became the leader and followed in his brother's wicked footsteps. Both of these men were born as Nephites but left their people and the Church. These brothers caused a lot of deaths and destruction. Their goals were to destroy the freedom of the Nephites and to make war against righteous people.

 Amalickiah's rebellion among the Nephites is what caused Captain Moroni to make the Title of Liberty.

 The Lord protected the Nephites due to their righteousness, and they enjoyed some of their happiest and most prosperous times even while these brothers were warring against them.

 Amalickiah became king of the Lamanites around 73 BC.

 Teancum, the Nephite military hero, snuck into the Lamanite camp two different times to defeat Amalickiah and then later Ammoron.

 "Yea, and we also see the great wickedness one very wicked man can cause to take place among the children of men" (Alma 46:9).

Me! Me! Me! (Alma 46–54)

All of the problems that Amalickiah and Ammoron caused for themselves, their followers, and the righteous Nephites began when Amalickiah decided he wanted to become king and rule over the Nephites. When Captain Moroni stopped him, Amalickiah became very angry and decided to spend the rest of his life seeking revenge. He lied and murdered so that he could obtain the power he wanted. His greed ruined a lot of peoples' lives. After Amalickiah died, his brother Ammoron took over and spent all of his energy trying to seek revenge for his brother.

"I will come upon you with my armies. . . . And we will wage a war which shall be eternal." (Alma 54:16, 20)

Ammoron lived out the rest of his life in misery like his brother had. Both of these men had very sad stories. They were greedy, wanted revenge, and did not care about anyone except themselves. This made them angry and miserable.

A heart that is filled with selfishness, revenge, and anger can never be happy. There are a lot of opportunities to think only about yourself. If we forget the commandment to love our neighbor, our life will be very lonely and sad.

? Will you fight against the desire to be selfish in your daily life? When is the last time you thought about the happiness of someone else before your own?

Activity

Have everyone in the family dedicate one day of the coming week to be a "Make everyone else happy day." Encourage family members to try to make every decision that day based on the needs or wants of someone else. At the end of the chosen day, have everyone report on their experiences and feelings.

Lehonti

Lamanite

Lehonti was a Lamanite soldier and leader who was murdered after he fell for a trick laid by the wicked Nephite Amalickiah. When Amalickiah failed in his goal to take over the Nephite government, he decided to try to take over as king of the Lamanites. Amalickiah convinced the king of the Lamanites to go to war with the Nephites, but many of the Lamanite soldiers were afraid and did not want to go. Lehonti led the group of Lamanites who did not want to go to war. The king sent Amalickiah to convince Lehonti's group to join them. Eventually Amalickiah tricked Lehonti into thinking they were friends, killed Lehonti, and took over his army.

 Lehonti's group fled to a mountaintop called Mount Antipas to avoid a war with the Nephites.

 Amalickiah tricked Lehonti into making him second in command in his army. Under Lamanite law, if the first in command dies, the second in command takes over.

 Lehonti was killed by poison given to him a little at a time by a servant of Amalickiah.

 "And it came to pass that when Lehonti received the message he durst not go down to the foot of the mount. And it came to pass that Amalickiah sent again the second time" (Alma 47:11).

Stay on the Mount (Alma 47)

When Lehonti led a group of Lamanites who didn't want to go to war with the Nephites, the king sent Amalickiah to retrieve them. Lehonti took his group to a safe spot on the mountaintop. Amalickiah tried to get Lehonti to come down and talk to him three different times, but Lehonti refused. The fourth time, Amalickiah went closer to the group's camp, where Lehonti would be more comfortable, and promised him safety. Lehonti gave in. Amalickiah flattered and tricked Lehonti into putting him second in command.

"And it came to pass that Amalickiah caused that one of his servants should administer poison by degrees to Lehonti, that he died." (Alma 47:18)

Amalickiah gradually convinced Lehonti to come down from his safe place and then slowly killed him with poison. Lehonti died without even knowing he was ever in danger.

This is the same way the devil works on us. He tries to get us to make small decisions that lower our standards. He makes us feel safe and convinces us to commit small sins. If Lehonti would have stayed on the mountaintop, he would have been safe. We can learn from this sad story to never come down from our spiritual safe places.

? What will you do when you are tempted to lower your standards, even just a little? What will you do to stay spiritually safe?

Activity

Find or make a small container that will float in a bathtub or pool. After seeing it float, poke or drill a small hole into it, and then put it back in the water. What happens to the container? Talk about how the smallest holes can sink a ship, just like the smallest sins can sink a life.

Teancum

Nephite

Teancum was a strong and righteous captain in the Nephite army. He fought under the command of Chief Captain Moroni in the great wars against the Lamanites. Teancum was very diligent in everything he did to defend and protect the Nephites. Many of the smaller battles fought during these war times involved Teancum. He moved from place to place and found creative and clever ways to defeat the Lamanite armies. Teancum is responsible for the death of several wicked leaders who opposed the Nephites' freedom. When a job needed to be done, Teancum did not wait for someone else to do it. He was killed in the service of his people and his God.

Teancum led armies from about 67 BC to 60 BC, almost the length of the entire war.

At one point, Teancum and Lehi, another Nephite captain, were given command of the whole Nephite army.

Teancum snuck into a Lamanite city to kill the wicked king Amalickiah in his tent in the middle of the night.

Teancum also snuck into the tent of Amalickiah's brother Ammoron. He killed Ammoron, but Ammoron's servants woke up before Teancum could get away, and he was killed.

"For behold, he had been a man who had fought valiantly for his country, yea, a true friend to liberty; and he had suffered very many exceedingly sore afflictions" (Alma 62:37).

Valiantly (Alma 51–62)

From the very beginning of the war, Teancum spent all of his days fighting for the Nephites. He never complained through the struggles and battles. When Teancum was involved in a conflict, he worked hard and fought until it was over. He never gave up on the job of defending the liberty and the freedoms of the people. He always trusted Moroni and followed his orders. If there was a problem, Teancum would counsel with other captains about ways to solve it. The Lamanite armies did not like him, because he was such a valiant military leader.

"For every man of Teancum did exceed the Lamanites in their strength and in their skill of war." (Alma 51:31)

Teancum wanted to always be a force for good in the fight against the Lamanite armies.

There are many "Teancums" today who help in the fight for good and against evil. They solve problems, support their leaders, and are always trying to become stronger and better. They take action when they see a need. They look for ways to build, defend, and strengthen others.

? Will you fight valiantly in the battle against sin and evil? Will you be active in doing good?

Activity

Watch or attend a team sport event. Have everyone watch for a player or coach who acts like Teancum. Which person is giving his or her full effort and never gives up? Talk about playing on the Lord's team and giving the same type of effort.

Helaman

 **Nephite**

Helaman was the oldest son of Alma the Younger and was a righteous and powerful leader in the Church and the Nephite army. Helaman had three major jobs: take care of the records and other sacred things, build up the Church, and defend the Nephite cities against the attacking Lamanites. Chief Captain Moroni trusted Helaman, and they thought a lot alike. Neither of them wanted to go to war with the Lamanites but wanted to preserve peace and freedom. Helaman was a great strength in the wars against the Lamanites. One of the things he is known for is commanding the two thousand stripling warrior sons of the Anti-Nephi-Lehies. After the wars, Helaman returned to his work building up the Church and serving missions.

 While Moroni defended the Nephite cities, Helaman continued to build up the Church until he joined Moroni in the war.

 Helaman's brothers were Shiblon and Corianton. Helaman gave the plates to Shiblon before he died. Shiblon later gave them to Helaman's son, also named Helaman.

 The two thousand stripling warriors chose Helaman to be their leader and were known as the sons of Helaman.

 Miraculously, none of the two thousand stripling warriors Helaman led were killed.

 "Helaman and his brethren were no less serviceable unto the people than was Moroni; for they did preach the word of God, and they did baptize unto repentance all men whosoever would hearken unto their words" (Alma 48:19).

I Would Not Suffer (Alma 56)

The people of Ammon, or the Anti-Nephi-Lehies, made a covenant when they were converted that they would never use their weapons again to fight in battle. They buried their weapons and moved to a land next to the Nephites so they could be protected from danger. The Nephites were very kind and helpful to the Anti-Nephi-Lehies. When the Lamanites started attacking the Nephites, the Anti-Nephi-Lehies felt compassion for them and wanted to help.

"They were about to break the covenant which they had made. . . . But I would not suffer them that they should break this covenant which they had made, supposing that God would strengthen us." (Alma 56:7–8)

The Nephites really needed extra help in the battle he was fighting, but Helaman was more concerned about the Anti-Nephi-Lehies keeping their covenants. He cared about them and loved them. He would not allow them to break their promises, and he convinced them to stay true. When their sons volunteered to fight in their place, Helaman lovingly led and cared for them as if they were his own sons.

Everyone needs a family member, leader, or friend like Helaman. There are so many excuses for breaking covenants, and we need someone who will watch over us and help us keep our covenants no matter what. We need to do that for others as well.

? Will you be like Helaman and speak up when those you love are tempted to break their covenants and promises? Will you do it even when it is not convenient or easy?

Activity

Draw sixteen boxes on a piece of paper and put a small piece of candy or cereal in each of the boxes. Choose someone to leave the room, and have everyone else choose which box contains "the poison." When the person returns, let him or her choose one candy at a time to eat. Everyone else watches closely to ensure the person doesn't eat "the poison." The person can keep eating the candy until he or she picks the poison square. When he or she chooses "the poison," everyone else yells "STOP!" to warn about "the poison." Let everyone have a turn. As a family, discuss ways to warn one another of spiritual dangers.

The Mothers of the Stripling Warriors

 Anti-Nephi-Lehies There were many people who listened to the teachings of Ammon and his brothers and joined the Church among the Lamanites. This converted group gathered together and called themselves the Anti-Nephi-Lehies. The faithful mothers and women of this group gave great strength to the men and boys in their families. These women joined with their husbands and families and made covenants to follow the Lord and leave behind their old, wicked ways. They trained their children to believe in the Lord, His prophets, and the power of miracles. The righteous way they raised their children became a great strength to the Nephites in their time of need.

 The sons of these mothers are known as the two thousand stripling warriors.

These women and their husbands made a covenant of peace as they buried their weapons of war when they converted to the gospel.

 None of the women who joined the Church and followed the teachings of Ammon ever fell away.

 The Anti-Nephi-Lehies lived in the land of Jershon and were protected by the Nephites. When the Nephites were under attack, the Anti-Nephi-Lehies wanted to help them and almost broke their covenants in order to fight the Lamanites.

 "And they rehearsed unto me the words of their mothers, saying: We do not doubt our mothers knew it" (Alma 56:48).

Our Mothers Knew It (Alma 53-57)

When the wicked Lamanite armies began their attack, the Nephites found they were in a time of great trouble and needed help. The Anti-Nephi-Lehies had buried their weapons of war and made a covenant never to fight, so their sons stepped up to help their parents and the Nephites.

"Now they never had fought, yet they did not fear death; . . . yea, they had been taught by their mothers, that if they did not doubt, God would deliver them." (Alma 56:47)

Long before these young men volunteered to fight, they had been taught very important lessons by their mothers. Their mothers taught them to believe in a God of miracles. They taught their sons to fear sin but not to fear hard things. They taught them to be faithful and true at all times. They taught them to pray and to trust God. Day after day, these mothers taught their children through their words and example. When the time for battle arrived, their sons were ready.

We live in times of great trouble today. There are many things that threaten our faith and our families. We will all need to battle for ourselves and others. We need mothers like these great women to teach and prepare their children for the future. We need children to listen and trust the lessons of their mothers.

? Will you prepare for the future battles you face by listening to the words of your mother and other faithful women?

Activity

Have everyone write a letter to their mother or another faithful woman who has influenced them. Encourage everyone to write or draw something to show appreciation for what these righteous women have taught them. What difference have these women made in your family members' lives? Perhaps you could review some of the things the Anti-Nephi-Lehi mothers taught their children for ideas.

Two Thousand Stripling Warriors

 **Anti-Nephi-Lehies**

Two of the most famous battles in the Book of Mormon involved a group of two thousand young men called the stripling warriors. The stripling warriors are some of the sons of the Anti-Nephi-Lehies. Their fathers and mothers converted to the Lord after Ammon the missionary taught among their people. These faithful parents made covenants with God never to go to war again. When the Nephite armies needed help, these young men stepped up to fight in place of their fathers. The young men had never fought before, but they made a great difference in the wars between the Nephites and the Lamanites and helped the Nephites win.

 Two thousand young men came to fight in the stripling warriors' first battle. In a later battle, sixty more joined them.

 In the second battle, every stripling warrior was injured, but miraculously not one of them died in either battle.

 The word *stripling* means young.

 The stripling warriors are also known as the army of Helaman or the sons of Helaman, because they chose Helaman to be their leader and captain.

 "And now, their preservation was astonishing to our whole army, . . . and we do justly ascribe it to the miraculous power of God, because of their exceeding faith in that which they had been taught to believe" (Alma 57:26).

Exceedingly Valiant (Alma 53–56)

After the two battles the stripling warriors fought in, Helaman was overjoyed to learn that none of them had died. Not one! It was a miracle. This was a special experience, but these soldiers were also special young men.

"And they were all young men, and they were exceedingly valiant for courage, and also for strength and activity; but behold, this was not all—they were men who were true at all times in whatsoever thing they were entrusted." (Alma 53:20)

These young men had been taught by their parents to be obedient with exactness and to always do what the Lord wanted them to do. No matter what situation they were in, they stayed true to what they knew was right. They always gave the Lord their very best. They tried to be perfectly honest, loving, and valiant. They were not perfect, but they made sure their parents and their Heavenly Father would be pleased with the way they acted.

In every situation, we have the opportunity to live like the stripling warriors did—valiant, upright, and true at all times. We can commit to giving our very best to the Lord.

? Will you make it your quest to be as good and faithful as you can? Will you valiantly serve and love? Will you always give the Lord the best that you have?

Activity

As a family, read Alma 53:20–21 and make a list of the attributes of the stripling warriors. Talk about each quality and what a modern stripling warrior would look like in everyday situations. How would they act at school or work? How would they spend their free time? Invite family members to think of people they know who are a good example of each of the attributes and to share how those people bless others.

Pahoran

 **Nephite**

Pahoran was the third chief judge over the Nephites and was a wonderful, righteous, and Christlike leader. He was the chief judge during some very difficult days. During his time as chief judge, a group of people known as the "king-men" tried to overthrow Pahoran, take over the government, and choose a king to be their leader instead. Pahoran fought for the rights of the people, but at one point during the rebellion he was overthrown. Captain Moroni came to his rescue. Pahoran was also the chief judge during the great wars with the Lamanites. He is a perfect example of a leader with great strength and Christlike humility.

 Pahoran became the chief judge after his father Nephihah around 68 BC.

 Mormon included in The Book of Mormon three letters sent between Helaman, Moroni, and Pahoran that show what kind of man Pahoran was.

 While the Nephite armies were off at war with the Lamanites, a group called the king-men invaded the capital city and kicked Pahoran out, knowing there was nobody in the city to defend him.

 Pahoran had many sons. When he died, three of them argued for the position of chief judge. His son Pahoran was elected, but the followers of one of the other sons had him killed.

 "And those who were desirous that Pahoran should remain chief judge over the land took upon them the name of freemen; . . . for the freemen had sworn or covenanted to maintain their rights and the privileges of their religion by a free government" (Alma 51:6).

Turn the Other Cheek (Alma 59–61)

Toward the end of the great wars with the Lamanites, Moroni sent a letter to Pahoran in the capital asking him for help defending the Nephite cities. When no help came and the Lamanites attacked the cities, Moroni was very sad and angry. He thought that Pahoran was being lazy and not doing his job. Captain Moroni called Pahoran a traitor and threatened to march his army to the capital to punish Pahoran if he did not help the Nephite armies. What Moroni did not know was that Pahoran had been chased out of the city and was in serious trouble himself. Even though Moroni was a bit harsh in his letter, Pahoran responded with kindness.

"You have censured me, but it mattereth not; I am not angry, but do rejoice in the greatness of your heart." (Alma 61:9)

Pahoran could have been very angry with Moroni for his letter. He could have taken offense and written a nasty letter back to Moroni. Moroni made a mistake in his letter, but Pahoran immediately forgave him.

Whether on purpose or by accident, people may do things that hurt your feelings, are unfair, or are unkind. You have a choice to respond in anger or respond like Pahoran, assuming the best and quickly forgiving.

? Will you be quick to assume the best in people?
Will you offer your forgiveness freely?

Activity

Have everyone turn to the topic of forgiveness in the Topical Guide of the scriptures. Ask everyone to find a scripture or story that demonstrates the importance of showing patience and forgiving others.

Samuel the Lamanite

Samuel the Lamanite was a righteous man and prophet of God who was sent to preach repentance to the city of Zarahemla. Throughout most of the Book of Mormon, the Lord had to send righteous Nephites to preach repentance to the Lamanites. However, a few years before the birth of Christ, the city of Zarahemla had become very wicked, and the Lord sent His servant Samuel to preach to the Nephites. The people of Zarahemla locked Samuel out of the city, so he climbed on top of the city walls to preach to them. He taught them many things, including signs to watch for that would mean Jesus Christ had been born. Most of the people did not believe him. They tried to kill him with arrows, but the Lord protected him. When he finished preaching his message, Samuel escaped from the wall and was never seen again by the people of Zarahemla.

 The Book of Mormon does not say where Samuel the Lamanite came from or anything about his family.

 Samuel came to the city of Zarahemla around 6 BC.

 Samuel prophesied about the many signs in heaven the people would see when Christ was born—including a new star.

 The prophet Nephi was living in Zarahemla during the time that Samuel came.

 "And it came to pass that they would not suffer that he should enter into the city; therefore he went and got upon the wall thereof, and stretched forth his hand and cried with a loud voice, and prophesied unto the people whatsoever things the Lord put into his heart" (Helaman 13:4).

One More Day (Helaman 13–16)

The Lord sent Samuel the Lamanite on a very difficult assignment to preach to the people of Zarahemla. The first time Samuel tried to teach the people, they kicked him out of their city. This must have been discouraging for Samuel. As he was returning to his home, the Lord spoke to him.

"But behold, the voice of the Lord came unto him, that he should return again, and prophesy unto the people whatsoever things should come into his heart." (Helaman 13:3)

When Samuel returned, he climbed to the top of the wall of the city to preach to the people. He taught the words that the Lord put into his heart. His words caused many people to repent. Others were angry and began to shoot arrows or throw rocks to knock him off the wall. The Lord protected Samuel so that none of the arrows or rocks could hit him. This convinced more people to repent.

You may sometimes want to give up when things get hard. The Lord wants you to stand up and fight for one more day. When you feel like you have failed, He wants you to return and try again. When you do, He will be by your side. He will strengthen you and protect you. You will never have to do His work alone.

? On the days when you want to give up, will you find the strength to stand up and fight for one more day? Will you promise to never give up on doing what is right?

Activity

As a family, act out the story of Samuel the Lamanite. Have someone stand on a chair or ladder and share some of the truths Samuel taught in Helaman chapters 13 through 16. Give everyone else crumpled up paper or tin foil to throw at Samuel on the wall. Make sure they know to miss! Talk about what you learn from Samuel about difficult assignments from the Lord.

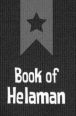
Nephi and Lehi

Nephite

Nephi and Lehi were brothers who were righteous missionaries and prophets. Their father was Helaman, who was the son of the Helaman who led the stripling warriors. They were powerful teachers and messengers for Jesus Christ. They were Nephites and lived and taught during a time when there was a lot of wickedness among the people. They each had powerful experiences teaching among the Lamanites and experienced great miracles. On one mission together, they baptized eight thousand Lamanites into the Church. Nephi was the head of the Church for a time and was very sad about the wickedness of the people. He was also the chief judge of the land, but he gave up that role to be a missionary for the Lord. Through the power of God, he performed miracles that convinced some people to change, but most of the people were very hard in their hearts.

 Nephi and Lehi lived during the time of the Gadianton robbers. The group of robbers caused a lot of difficulty for these righteous brothers.

 These two prophets were the grandsons of Captain Helaman, who was the son of Alma the Younger.

 The ministry of Nephi and Lehi took place from about 39 BC to AD 1—almost forty years!

 Nephi was very trusted by the Lord and was given the sealing power—the power to bind and loose things on earth and in heaven.

 "Blessed art thou, . . . for I have beheld how thou hast with unwearyingness declared the word, which I have given unto thee, unto this people. And thou hast not feared them, and hast not sought thine own life, but hast sought my will, and to keep my commandments. And now, because thou hast done this with such unwearyingness, behold, I will bless thee forever" (Helaman 10:4–5).

What's in a Name? (Helaman 5)

Nephi and Lehi were sons of a very righteous father. When Nephi and Lehi saw the wickedness of the people around them, they became very disheartened, but the words and teachings of their father gave them strength.

"Behold, my sons, . . . I have given unto you the names of our first parents who came out of the land of Jerusalem; and this I have done that when you remember your names ye may remember them; and when ye remember them ye may remember their works; and when ye remember their works ye may know how that it is said, . . . that they were good." (Helaman 5:6)

Their father's counsel motivated Nephi and Lehi to keep trying hard to be good and to live righteously. Many people fought against them, but Nephi and Lehi remembered who they represented, and it gave them strength to carry on.

Each of us has at least two important names. Each of us has a family name or surname. Wherever we go and whatever we do, we represent our families. We should bring honor to this name. We also have taken on us the name of Christ. We represent Him in all things. Like Nephi and Lehi, we can find strength and commitment when we think about the names that we have been given and what those names mean for us.

? Will you be true to the names that you bear? Will you live in a way that brings honor to your family and to the Savior?

Activity

Spend some time talking about the names of each family member and why those names were chosen. Did the name come from a family member, a friend, a scripture hero? Did it represent something special or just sound pretty? Show your family a missionary name tag (or a picture of one) and point out the name of Christ on it. Talk about what it means to wear His name as a full-time missionary and then all your life as one of His disciples.

Nephi, Son of Nephi

Nephi the prophet was a righteous Nephite who lived during a time of much trial, which led to a special time of great joy. Nephi was given responsibility over the sacred records and the Church when his father, Nephi, died. This was very close to the time that Christ was born in Bethlehem. For thirty years, Nephi lived in a civilization that was being destroyed through wickedness. The Gadianton robbers were pulling people away from their faith and killing the righteous. When the Savior died in the old world, there was great destruction in the Nephite lands, which destroyed the wicked people. Soon after this, the Savior came among the Nephites. He chose Nephi as the leader of His Church, and Nephi was a witness to all of the miracles and teachings of Jesus Christ's ministry in the new world.

 Because Nephi was in charge of the sacred records, all of the writings about Jesus Christ's ministry in Third Nephi were recorded by him.

 When the Savior came to the new world, Nephi was the first person called by name to come up and greet Him. He was one of the twelve disciples called by the Savior.

 Nephi is the second of three people in a row named Nephi. His father was Nephi, the prophet brother of Lehi. His son was also named Nephi.

 The Lord performed great miracles through Nephi, including raising his brother Timothy from the dead.

 "And Nephi did minister with power and with great authority. . . . For it were not possible that they could disbelieve his words, for so great was his faith on the Lord Jesus Christ that angels did minister unto him daily" (3 Nephi 7:17–18).

On This Night (3 Nephi 1)

Five years before Nephi became the head of the Church, the prophet Samuel prophesied of the sign of Christ's birth. The sign would be a day, a night, and another day passing with no darkness. Many people did not believe Samuel, but the faithful Nephites waited for the sign to come. As time passed, the wicked people set a date as a deadline for the sign. If the sign did not come by that day, they would kill the believers. The people looked to Nephi, the new leader of the Church, for strength and courage. Nephi was full of sorrow, but he told his people to trust in the Lord. He prayed all day, and then received his answer.

"Lift up your head and be of good cheer; for behold, the time is at hand, and on this night shall the sign be given, and on the morrow come I into the world." (3 Nephi 1:13)

Just when the faithful were about to lose hope, the sign came and they were saved.

There will be miracles you will want and wait for in your life. Sometimes they will come quickly, and sometimes they will require great patience. But eventually, all people who trust in the Lord receive the blessings they are promised—in this life or the next. When the Savior came among the Nephites after His Resurrection, he called Nephi to come forth, and He will call forth all of us. We must stay true and faithful until that day.

? Will you continue to hope for good things to come? Will you faithfully wait on the Lord and believe in the great things He has promised?

Activity

Have everyone in the family write down one miracle or blessing they are waiting and hoping for, and then share what you each wrote down. If possible, go online and watch the Mormon Message video "Good Things to Come" to hear Elder Jeffrey R. Holland's testimony about hope and faith.

The Gadianton Robbers

The Gadianton robbers were a group of wicked men and women who caused a lot of sorrow among the people of the Book of Mormon. The group was made up of both Nephites and Lamanites and was named after Gadianton, the evil man who was the group's second leader. Their goal was to gain money and power. They committed many crimes to get what they wanted and promised to keep their evil deeds a secret among their group. The Gadianton robbers varied in number and strength over time. At times the group would be destroyed, but then someone else would start it again. This evil group of people eventually destroyed the Nephite nation.

 The secrets that united the Gadianton robbers were called "secret combinations."

 The first crime of the group was the murder of the chief judge Paanchi by a man named Kishkumen. Gadianton took over leadership of the group when Kishkumen died.

 The group was destroyed during the destruction that came with the Savior's death, but the group was organized again in AD 260.

 A similar group with the same type of secrets and evil goals existed among the Jaredites in the Book of Ether.

 "And behold, in the end of this book ye shall see that this Gadianton did prove the overthrow, yea, almost the entire destruction of the people of Nephi" (Helaman 2:13).

Dangerous Secrets (Helaman 6)

There were many times when the Nephites and Lamanites had to deal with the Gadianton robbers. The Gadianton robbers grew stronger when the people were more wicked. When the people repented and turned to the Lord, the Gadianton robbers grew weak.

"And it came to pass that the Lamanites did hunt the band of robbers of Gadianton; and they did preach the word of God among the more wicked part of them, insomuch that this band of robbers was utterly destroyed from among the Lamanites." (Helaman 6:37)

Most of the acts of the Gadianton robbers were done in secret, so the people let them happen. The Lamanites, however, knew the robbers were dangerous, so they went after them.

Satan wants us to hide our sins from people who could help us. We should treat the sins and temptations in our lives the same way the Lamanites treated the Gadianton robbers. Search for parts of your life that might not be worthy or right. Do not keep secrets about inappropriate actions or hide bad choices. If you do, those things might ruin you.

? Will you watch your thoughts, words, and actions carefully? Are there wrong choices and secret sins that you need to get rid of?

Activity

Gather together a large number of socks, beanbags, or other small, soft items. Make two teams, and draw a dividing line in a room. Give each team an equal number of socks or beanbags. Begin a timer, then have each team try to throw their items out of their side of the room and into the other. When the timer stops, whoever has the most items on their side loses. Talk about how diligent we must be in order to remove sin from our lives. We must constantly throw out sin if we want to be victorious.

Mormon

Mormon is one of the last prophets of the Book of Mormon. He was commanded to gather the writings of every other prophet and put them together into one record. Mormon was given his special calling and mission when he was only ten years old. Throughout his life, he witnessed wars and much wickedness. Mormon was a tenderhearted man, but he was asked to lead the armies of the Nephites for many years. He was reluctant to lead the armies because the people were so wicked and refused to repent. Mormon watched the destruction of the Nephites at the end of his life. He gave the gold plates to his son, Moroni, before he was killed.

 The prophet Ammaron told Mormon about the place of records when Mormon was only ten years old but told him not to go there until he was twenty-four.

 Mormon was asked to be the leader of the Nephite armies when he was sixteen years old.

 In his teenage years, Mormon was already very close to the Lord. He was visited by the Savior when he was fifteen years old.

 Mormon was named after his father and the land of Mormon. The land of Mormon is the place where Alma took his followers and baptized them after they escaped from wicked King Noah.

 "Behold, I am a disciple of Jesus Christ, the Son of God. I have been called of him to declare his word among his people, that they might have everlasting life" (3 Nephi 5:13).

For Our Day (Mormon)

Every person who loves the messages and stories of the Book of Mormon needs to thank Mormon. He spent countless hours reading through the ancient records, editing, and writing to create the gold plates the Book of Mormon was translated from. He took one thousand years' worth of records and chose the parts that would be the most helpful for people in our day. None of the people in the Book of Mormon were able to read his abridgement. It was put together for us.

"Therefore I write unto you, . . . behold, I write unto all the ends of the earth." (Mormon 3:17–18)

Mormon gave his life so that we could have this special book. He could only include a small portion of all the writings that were in his possession. He prayed and fasted to know which parts would best help us live valiantly in the time before the Second Coming of Christ.

As you read the Book of Mormon, you might want to think about why Mormon chose to include some of the testimonies and stories. How can they help you? How can they help people that you know?

? Will you make studying the Book of Mormon an important part of your life? Will you share the messages it teaches with other people who need the truth and help it can give?

Activity

Gather together many pictures of stories from the Book of Mormon. Perhaps you want to look through this book to see pictures of the different heroes and villains and the lessons we learn from them. Let each person in the family tell about his or her favorite person or lesson from the Book of Mormon and why that person or lesson is meaningful.

Jared

Jared was a righteous man who left the Tower of Babel with a group of people to live in the promised land. Jared and his family arrived in the promised land many hundreds of years before the family of Lehi did. Jared and his brother lived near the Tower of Babel when the Lord confused all the languages and scattered people everywhere. Jared's brother was a righteous man and prophet who helped to lead the group in barges, or small boats, across the ocean. The Lord guided Jared's family to the promised land and sent prophets among his descendants for many years. The record of these people is found in the Book of Ether.

 The group that went with Jared and their descendants are known as the Jaredites.

 The record of the Jaredites was written on twenty-four gold plates discovered by the people of Limhi after the Jaredites had all died.

 Jared had twelve children—eight daughters and four sons.

 The Jaredites wanted to have a king. They asked for one of the sons of Jared or his brother to rule, but all the sons refused except one—Orihah.

 "There will I bless thee and thy seed, and raise up unto me of thy seed, and of the seed of thy brother, and they who shall go with thee, a great nation. And there shall be none greater than the nation which I will raise up unto me" (Ether 1:43).

Be a "Possibilitarian" (Ether 1–2)

When the people of Babel tried to build a tower to reach heaven, the Lord confused their languages so they couldn't understand one another. Jared knew that his brother was a great prophet and asked him to plead with the Lord not to confuse their family's languages. The Lord had compassion on them answered their plea. Jared then asked his brother to ask the Lord if he would spare their families and friends. The Lord also answered that prayer.

"And who knoweth but the Lord will carry us forth into a land which is choice above all the earth?" (Ether 1:38)

When the group was in a time of potential trouble, Jared asked the Lord for help. He asked for the very best things he could think of. He knew that God was a loving Father and would be willing to give the righteous all that He could. Jared believed anything was possible with God. He was a "possibilitarian."

The Lord is willing to bless us, but sometimes those blessings are only given if we ask for them. Heavenly Father loves us and is able to do anything for us if it is His will. We can ask Him for the very best blessings and miracles.

? Will you seek the blessings of the Lord in all that you do? Will you seek for and live for His greatest blessings?

Activity

Set out an ice cream sundae bar. Bring ice cream and several candies and other toppings. Let everyone order what they want. Explain that they should order their very favorite and create the best dessert possible for them. Explain that the Lord is often willing to bless us with the very best that He can if we will ask Him.

The Brother of Jared

The brother of Jared was a man of great faith. Jared and his brother were living near the Tower of Babel when the Lord confused the people's languages. The Lord guided the brother of Jared to lead a group of people out of the Old World and toward the promised land. The brother of Jared was a man of great faith, and he communicated with the Lord often. On one occasion, he was able to see and talk with the premortal Savior because of his faith in the Lord. The Lord tutored the brother of Jared and used him to perform many miracles and teach many truths.

 The scriptures do not tell us the brother of Jared's name, but Joseph Smith revealed that it was Mahonri Moriancumer.

 The Lord spoke with the brother of Jared for three hours and chastened, or corrected, him for not praying regularly.

 The Jaredites' journey across the sea to the promised land took about 344 days.

 In the promised land, the brother of Jared performed many miracles, including moving the mountain Zerin out of its place.

 "Never has man come before me with such exceeding faith as thou hast; for were it not so ye could not have seen my finger. . . . And never have I showed myself unto man whom I have created, for never has man believed in me as thou hast" (Ether 3:9,15).

Prepared for the Journey (Ether 2–3)

The Jaredite barges faced three problems. They had no steering wheel, air, or light. The brother of Jared went to the Lord to get help. In answer to his prayer, the Lord gave the brother of Jared solutions to his first two problems. The Lord would steer them through the ocean by His mighty hand, and He showed the brother of Jared how to cut holes for air. When the brother of Jared asked again about light, the Lord responded,

"What will ye that I should do that ye may have light in your vessels?" (Ether 2:23)

The Lord gave the brother of Jared the responsibility to think and do his part in bringing about a miracle. The brother of Jared gathered sixteen white stones from a high mountain, purified them with fire, and then carried them again to a high place. In great faith, the brother of Jared asked the Lord to touch the stones so they would shine brightly. The Lord touched the stones, and the people had light.

The brother of Jared showed both effort and great faith in the Lord.

As we seek the Lord's help in our lives, we should remember to do everything in our power to obtain what we need. As we act in faith, the Lord will bless our efforts, as He did with the brother of Jared.

? Are you willing to do all that you can when you take your questions and problems to the Lord? Will you show your faith and desire by doing your part?

Activity

Have everyone in the family search outdoors for a small, smooth rock. Clean them and paint them white. Have everyone put their rocks in their rooms or in another place where they can see them as reminders of God's miracles and the importance of showing our faith and desire through our efforts.

Ether

Ether was called to be a prophet and preach repentance to the Jaredites, who had become very wicked after many generations of living in the promised land. He was the last prophet of the Jaredite nation before they were destroyed. His record is called the Book of Ether. The Lord commanded Ether to tell the king, Coriantumr, that if he and his family repented, the people would be spared. But if they didn't repent, the entire nation would be destroyed, and Coriantumr would only live long enough to see another people take possession of the land. The king did not believe Ether and refused to repent. The people tried to kill Ether, but he hid from them. The Jaredites continued to fight among themselves until Coriantumr was the only one left alive. Ether's prophecy had been fulfilled, and the Jaredite people met their end.

 The prophet Moroni abridged the record of the prophet Ether.

 Ether's record was kept on twenty-four gold plates that the people of Limhi later discovered.

 The Urim and Thummim that Joseph Smith used to translate the Book of Mormon came from the Jaredites.

 Ether prophesied and taught boldly on many topics, including faith and hope.

 "And Ether was a prophet of the Lord . . . and began to prophesy unto the people, for he could not be restrained because of the Spirit of the Lord which was in him. For he did cry from morning, even until the going down of the sun, exhorting the people to believe in God" (Ether 12:2–3).

A Lonely Disciple (Ether 12–14)

The prophet Ether was called to prophesy and teach a very stubborn and wicked people. He taught the people from morning until night. Everywhere he went, people rejected his message. Eventually, the people got so wicked that Ether's life was in danger.

"They esteemed him as naught, and cast him out; and he hid himself in the cavity of a rock by day, and by night he went forth . . . viewing the destruction which came upon the people." (Ether 13:13–14)

Ether was trying to help the people, but they did not want anything to do with him. They even tried to kill him for what he said. He was forced to hide in a cave during the day for protection. His choice to help other people left him sad and lonely. Ether knew that sometimes being a disciple requires sacrifice.

There will be times when you want to help people but they will not listen. Some of them may make fun of you or treat you badly. Following the Savior may even mean you lose some friends and face some lonely days. Even if this happens, the Lord will never leave you alone. He knows how you feel and will comfort and love you for your sacrifice.

? Will you take the difficult and sometimes lonely path to be a disciple of Jesus Christ? Will you reach out to rescue others even when they reject you?

Activity

Have everyone write a letter of encouragement to themselves or someone else in the family. Write about how much Heavenly Father loves His children and why it is worth it to keep going. Seal the letter and write over the seal, "For days when it is lonely and hard." Have everyone keep their letters somewhere safe until a day they need to open it.

Moroni

Nephite

Moroni was the final prophet of the Book of Mormon prophets. He was also the last living Nephite on the earth. He was the son of Mormon and was put in charge of the gold plates—the record which was translated into the Book of Mormon—when his father died. After he received the plates, Moroni wrote a few more teachings from his father and his final testimony before burying the plates in the ground. His final teachings about the gifts of the Spirit and faith, hope, and charity are some of the most wonderful and beautiful truths in the book. After many years, Moroni returned as an angel to the Prophet Joseph Smith to tutor him and direct him in the translation of the record he had buried. It was published as the Book of Mormon in 1830.

 Moroni wandered alone as the last Nephite for more than thirty years. During those years he was chased by Lamanite warriors.

 Moroni wrote his final words and then buried the plates around AD 421.

 Moroni was most likely named after Chief Captain Moroni, a man his father had admired and loved very much.

 Moroni was privileged to see the Savior face to face in his lifetime. He bore a powerful testimony of Him.

 "Yea, come unto Christ, and be perfected in him, and deny yourselves of all ungodliness; and if ye shall deny yourselves of all ungodliness, and love God with all your might, mind and strength, then is his grace sufficient for you, that by his grace ye may be perfect in Christ; and if by the grace of God ye are perfect in Christ, ye can in nowise deny the power of God" (Moroni 10:32).

By the Power of the Holy Ghost (Moroni 10)

Before Moroni buried the plates in a hill, he wrote a personal message to every person who would ever read the Book of Mormon. While he was alive, Moroni received a vision of the people who would live in the last days. He knew the trials we would face, and he knew the Book of Mormon would get us through.

"And when ye shall receive these things, I would exhort you that ye would ask God, the Eternal Father, in the name of Christ, if these things are not true; and if ye shall ask with a sincere heart, with real intent, having faith in Christ, he will manifest the truth of it unto you, by the power of the Holy Ghost." (Moroni 10:4)

Moroni promised that everyone who reads and prays about the Book of Mormon can know it is true.

Take Moroni's challenge and read the Book of Mormon. Every time you read it, you can feel the truth of it through the Holy Ghost.

? Will you put Moroni's promise to the test? Will you read with a sincere heart and pray to know if the Book of Mormon truly is what it says it is—the word of God?

Activity

Obtain a missionary copy of the Book of Mormon for every member of the family. Have each person write down his or her feelings and testimony of the Book of Mormon in the front pages. Consider including a favorite verse. Have family members sign and date their writings. They can keep the copy of the Book of Mormon, or perhaps someday they will be prompted to pass it on to someone.

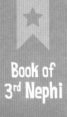

Jesus Christ

Jesus Christ is the Savior and Redeemer of the world. He is our older brother and the Son of our Heavenly Father. Jesus Christ suffered for all of our sins and pains and died on the cross for each of us. He was resurrected three days later in great glory. Christ's suffering and Resurrection is called the Atonement. Because of the Savior's Atonement, all mankind may be forgiven of their sins and will live again in a perfect resurrected body. After the Savior's Resurrection in Jerusalem, He visited the people of the Book of Mormon on the American continent. The record of His visit is the central part of the Book of Mormon.

 Jesus Christ visited the people of the Book of Mormon in a place called Bountiful.

 The Savior called twelve disciples and established His Church when He came to the American continent.

 A teaching about Jesus Christ can be found on nearly every page of the Book of Mormon.

 A record of Jesus Christ's teachings and miracles and ministry among the Nephites and Lamanites is found in Third Nephi.

 "And now, I would commend you to seek this Jesus of whom the prophets and apostles have written, that the grace of God the Father, and also the Lord Jesus Christ, and the Holy Ghost, which beareth record of them, may be and abide in you forever. Amen" (Ether 12:41).

A Happier People (3 Nephi 11–4 Nephi)

Every prophet of the Book of Mormon bore witness and testimony of Jesus Christ. The subtitle of the Book of Mormon says that the book is "Another Testament of Jesus Christ." The whole purpose of the book is to testify of and bring people closer to Christ. Only through Him can we return to Heavenly Father and enjoy eternal life. During the Savior's visit to the Americas, the people witnessed miracles and learned much from Him. Even after He left, their life was better than it had ever been.

"And it came to pass that there was no contention in the land, because of the love of God which did dwell in the hearts of the people. And there were no envyings, nor strifes, nor tumults, . . . and surely there could not be a happier people among all the people who had been created by the hand of God. There were no robbers, nor murderers, neither were there Lamanites, nor any manner of -ites; but they were in one, the children of Christ, and heirs to the kingdom of God." (4 Nephi 1:15–17)

When people follow the teachings and example of Jesus Christ, they experience happiness and joy that cannot come in any other way.

? Will you try to be like Jesus Christ every day? Will you strive to come unto Him throughout your life?

Activity

Watch the video "The Testaments: Of One Fold and One Shepherd" (you can find it online or watch the DVD). Or, review general conference talks to read the testimonies of living prophets and apostles about our Savior, Jesus Christ. Afterward, share your testimonies of Christ with one another and talk about what He has meant to you and your family.

Meet the Author and Illustrator

By day **David Butler** is a high school religious educator and has taught many students his love for the scriptures and the innate power for good in every human soul. By night he is a fort builder, waffle maker, sports coach, and storyteller for his five favorite little people. Somewhere in between those jobs he is a motivational speaker and writer. Some of his musings and challenges can be found on his blog, multiplygoodness.com. His darling wife, Jenny, and their five kids live in the snowy Mountain West, but they continually dream of a beach house on a sunny shore somewhere.

Ryan Jeppesen cultivated his love for art while growing up on a dairy farm in northern Utah. Ryan graduated from Utah State University with a bachelor's degree in marketing and a master's of business administration degree. He spends his days working at a cushy desk job and comes home at night to fully unleash his creativity by painting, drawing, illustrating, building websites, wood carving, toy building, sculpting, bread baking, and helping with countless Primary projects. He and his amazing wife, Brooke, are raising their four "Jeppesenite" children in the snowy cities of the Mountain West . . . and they like it there.